世界微型小说精选
译趣坊
张白桦

如果事与愿违 请相信一定另有安排

【加】斯蒂芬·里柯克 等著
张白桦 译

诙谐卷（中英双语）

世界微型小说精选

中国国际广播出版社

图书在版编目（CIP）数据

如果事与愿违　请相信一定另有安排：英汉对照 /（加）斯蒂芬·里柯克等著；张白桦译. —北京：中国国际广播出版社，2019.9
（译趣坊. 世界微型小说精选）
ISBN 978-7-5078-4520-4

Ⅰ. ①如…　Ⅱ. ①斯…②张…　Ⅲ. ①小小说—小说集—加拿大—现代—汉、英　Ⅳ. ①I711.45

中国版本图书馆CIP数据核字（2019）第184342号

如果事与愿违　请相信一定另有安排（中英双语）

著　　者	［加］斯蒂芬·里柯克 等
译　　者	张白桦
策　　划	张娟平
责任编辑	高　婧　张娟平
版式设计	国广设计室
责任校对	张　娜

出版发行	中国国际广播出版社［010-83139469　010-83139489（传真）］
社　　址	北京市西城区天宁寺前街2号北院A座一层 邮编：100055
网　　址	www.chirp.com.cn
经　　销	新华书店
印　　刷	环球东方（北京）印务有限公司

开　　本	880×1230　1/32
字　　数	200千字
印　　张	7.5
版　　次	2019 年 10 月　北京第一版
印　　次	2019 年 10 月　第一次印刷
定　　价	28.00元

CRI　欢迎关注本社新浪官方微博
中国国际广播出版社　官方网站 www.chirp.cn

·代○序·

微型小说界的一个奇异存在

陈春水

张白桦，女，于1963年4月出生于辽宁沈阳一个世代书香的知识分子家庭，父亲是中国第一代俄语专业大学生。她曾先后就读于三所高校，具有双专业教育背景，所修专业分别为英国语言文学、比较文学与世界文学。两次跳级经历，一次是从初二到高三，一次是从大一到大二。最后学历为上海外国语大学文学硕士，研究方向为译介学，师从谢天振教授（国际知名比较文学专家与翻译理论家、译介学创始人、中国翻译学创建人、比较文学终身奖获得者），为英美文学研究专家、翻译家胡允桓（与杨宪益、沙博理、赵萝蕤、李文俊、董乐山同获“中美文学交流奖”，诺贝尔文学奖得主托妮·莫里森世界范围内研究兼汉译第一人，翻译终身奖获得者）私淑弟子。她现为内蒙古工业大学外国语学院副教授、硕士研究生导师，并兼任中国比较文学学会翻译研究会理事、上海翻译家协会会员、内蒙古作家协会会员。张白桦于1987年开始文学创作，已在《读者》《中外期刊文萃》《青年博览》《小小说选刊》《青年参考》《文学故事报》等海内外一百多种报刊，以及生活·读书·新知三联书店、中译出版社、北京大学出版社、中国国际广播出版社，公开出版以微型小说翻译为主，包括长篇小说、中篇小说、散文、随笔、诗歌、杂文、评论翻译和原创等在内的编著译作30部，累计1200万字。

在中国微型小说界，众所周知的是：以性别而论，男性译作者多，女性译作者少；以工作内容而论，搞创作的多，搞研究的少；以文学样式而论，只创作微型小说的作者多，同时创作长篇小说、散文、诗歌、文学评论的作者少；以作者性质而论，搞原创的多，搞翻译的少；以翻译途径而论，外译汉的译者多，汉译外的译者少；以译者而论，搞翻译的人多，同时搞原创的人少。而具备上述所有“少”于一身的奇异存在，恐怕张白桦是绝无仅有的一位。

张白桦是当代中国微型小说第一代译作者，也是唯一因微型小说翻译而获奖的翻译家。译作量大质优，覆盖面广泛，风格鲜明，具有女性文学史、微型小说史意义；是中国第一个从理论上，从宏观和微观层面，论证当代外国微型小说汉译的文学史意义的学者，具有翻译文学史意义；小说创作篇幅涉及长篇、中篇、短篇、微型小说，创作的文学样式覆盖小说、散文、诗歌、文学评论等主要文学样式；是既有微型小说译作，又有微型小说原创的全能型译作家，且译作与原创具有通约性；还是微型小说英汉双向翻译的译作者。

她的微型小说翻译实践开创了中国微型小说双向翻译的两个第一：“译趣坊”系列图书为中国首部微型小说译文集，在美国出版的《凌鼎年微型小说选集》为中国首部微型小说自选集英译本。

2002 年微型小说译著《英汉经典阅读系列散文卷》曾获上海外国语大学研究生学术文化节科研成果奖；1998 年微型小说译作《爱旅无涯》获《中国青年报·青年参考》最受读者喜爱的翻译文学作品；她本人曾在 2001 年当选小小说存档作家、2002 年当选为当代微型小说百家；微型小说译作《仇家》当选为全国第四次微型小说续写大赛竞赛原作；2012 年译作《海妖的诱惑》获以色列第 32 届世界诗人大会主席奖等文学奖项；“译趣坊”系列图书深受广大青年读者喜欢。

此外，她的论文《外国微型小说在中国的初期接受》入选复旦大学出版社的《润物有声——谢天振教授七十华诞纪念文集》，以及湖南大学出版社的张春的专著《中国小小说六十年》续表。译作《门把手》入选春风文艺出版社出版的《21 世纪中国文学大系 2002 年翻译文学》。译作《生命倒计时》入选春风文艺出版社出版的谢天振、韩忠良的专著《21 世纪中国文学大系 2010 年翻译文学》。

张白桦关于外国微型小说的论文具有前沿性和开拓意义。例如，《外国微型小说在中国的初期接受》是国内对于外国微型小说在中国接受的宏观梳理和微观分析。《当代外国微型小说汉译的文学史意义》证实了“微型小说翻译与微型小说原创具有同样建构民族、国别文学发展史的意义，即翻译文学应该，也只能是中国文学的一部分”。她指出，当代外国微型小说汉译的翻译文学意义在于：“推动中国当代的主流文学重归文学性，重归传统诗学的‘文以载道’的传统；引进并推动确立了一种新型的、活力四射的文学样式；当代微型小说汉译提高了文学的地位，直接催生并参与改写了中国当代文学史，以一种全新的文体重塑了当代主流诗学。”

其论文也反映出张白桦的文学翻译观和文学追求，例如，在《外国微型小说在中国的初期接受》中，她说：“吾以吾手译吾心。以文化和文学的传播为翻译的目的，以妇女儿童和青年为目标读者，让国人了解世界上其他民族的妇女儿童和青年的生存状态。以‘归化’为主，‘异化’为辅的翻译策略，全译为主，节译和编译为辅，突出译作的影响作用和感化作用，从而形成了简洁隽永、抒情、幽默、时尚的翻译风格。与此同时，译作与母语原创的微型小说，在思想倾向、语言要素、风格类型和审美趣味上形成了通约性和文化张力，丰富了译作的艺术表现力和感染力。”

在《当代外国微型小说汉译的文学史意义》中，她说：“文学翻译是创造性叛逆，创造性叛逆赋予原作以第二次生命，处于文学样式‘真空状态’的中国第一代微型小说译者一方面充分发挥了翻译的主体性作用，挥洒着‘创造性叛逆’所带来的‘豪杰’范儿，对于原文和原语文化‘傲娇’地‘引进并抵抗着’，有意和无意地遵循着自己的文学理想和审美趣味‘舞蹈’着，为翻译文学披上了‘中国红’的外衣，在内容和形式上赋予译作一种崭新的面貌和第二次生命。一方面在原文、意识形态、经济利益、诗学观念的‘镣铐’上，‘忠实’并‘妥协’着。”

著名评论家张锦贻在《亭亭白桦秀译林》中说：“张白桦所译的作品范围极广，涉及世界各大洲，但选择的标准却极严，注重原作表现生活的力度和反映社会的深度。显然，张白桦对于所译原作的这种选择，绝不仅仅是出于爱好，而是反映出她的审美意识和情感倾向。她着力在译作中揭示不同地区、不同国度、不同社会、不同人种的生存境况和心理状态，揭示东西方之间的文化差异和分歧，都显示出她是从人性和人道的角度来观察现实的人生。而正是通过这样的观察，才使她能够真正地去接触各国文学中那些反映社会底层的大众作品，才能使她真正地关注儿童和青年，也才使她的译作真正地走向中国的民众。事实证明，译作的高品位必伴以译者识见的高明和高超。脱了思想内核，怕是做不好文学译介工作的。……类似的译作比比皆是，到后来，就是事先不知道译者，几行读下来，亦能将她给‘认出来’。也就是说，张白桦在选择原作和自己的翻译文字上都在逐步形成一种独具的风格。……使她能够在不同的译作中巧用俚语，活用掌故，借用时俗。她善于用中国人最能领会的词语来表达各式各样的口吻，由此活现出不同人物的身份和此时此刻的心神和表情；她也长于用青少年最能领悟的词句来表达不同的侧面，同时展现出不同社会的氛围和当时当地的风习。”

胡晓在《中国教育报》发表的《学英语您捕捉到快乐了吗》:“我最喜欢她的译作，因为所选篇目均为凝练精巧之作，难易适中，且多是与生活息息相关的内容，能够极大限度地接近读者。所选的文字皆为沙里淘金的名家经典，文华高远，辞采华丽。名家的经典带来的是审美的享受和精神的愉悦，含蓄隽永的语句令人不由得会心一笑;至真至纯的爱与情，轻轻拨动着人们的神经;睿智透彻的思考，让人旷达而超脱。”

综上所述，在微型小说的文化地理中，张白桦是一个独特的所在。她以独特的文化品相，承接了中华与西洋的博弈，以理论和实践造就的衍生地带，自绘版图却无人能袭。

（作者系中国作协会员，小小说作家网特约评论家，第六届小小说金麻雀提名奖获得者，本篇原载于中国作家网 2015 年 9 月 9 日 http://www.chinawriter.com.cn）

代○序

没有微型小说汉译就没有当代微型小说

——张白桦访谈录

陈勇（中国作协会员，小小说作家网特约评论家，第六届小小说金麻雀提名奖获得者，以下简称陈）：我做微型小说评论多年，范围遍及世界华文微型小说界，您是我研究视野中出现的第一个微型小说翻译家，可能也是唯一的一个。

张白桦（以下简称张）：谢谢陈老师的青睐，我更加惊诧于您的学术识别力。因为，即使在外语界和翻译界，对于文学翻译的认识还是有许多误区的。难怪微型小说界的评论总是视译者为“局外人”，所以无人问津了。而从我的研究方向——译介学的角度来看，得出的结论是：微型小说翻译，特别是微型小说翻译文学，应该，也只是中国文学的一部分。

陈：我认同翻译与创作是国别文学的“鸟之两翼，车之两轮”之说，您能给大家普及一下文学翻译与文学创作的区别吗？

张：好的，我愿意。从文艺的本质规律来看，二者并没有分别。

从创作的内容来看，翻译的确比创作少了一道工序——构思。然而，也正是由于这一缺失，反而给翻译带来了创作所没有的困难。可以负责任地说，从创作的过程来看，正如许许多多20世纪三四十年代的作家兼翻译家共同体会到的那样，文学翻译比文学创作要难。

陈：我之所以选择了您作为评论对象，是由于您在微型小说界的独特地位和影响力，以及您在研究和实践层面的全面开花的成果。

张：这倒是符合事实的。在实践方面，我在20世纪80年代初，也就是大三的时候，就翻译了第一篇微型小说，一直走下来，应该说与当代中国微型小说是共同成长的，又是唯一一个因此获奖的译者；此外，中国首部微型小说译文集“译趣坊”系列图书和中国首部微型小说自选集英译本《凌鼎年微型小说选集》也是我做的。在研究方面，是中国第一个从理论上，从宏观和微观层面，论证当代外国微型小说汉译的文学史意义的学人。

陈：您能把您的理论观点论述得详细些吗？

张：可以，当代外国微型小说汉译的翻译文学意义就在于：推动中国当代的主流文学重归文学性，重归传统诗学的“文以载道”的传统；引进并推动确立了一种新型的、活力四射的文学样式；当代微型小说汉译提高了文学的地位，直接催生并参与改写了中国当代文学史，以一种全新的文体重塑了当代主流诗学。

陈：哦，所以您才会下这样的判断：“没有外国微型小说汉译，就没有当代微型小说。”是吗？

张：您的学术敏感度令人惊叹。

陈：根据我的调查统计分析，发现搞微型小说翻译实践的人虽然相对不多，却也还是有一些的，您能谈谈使您脱颖而出的“别裁之处”吗？

张：我是经历了实践—理论—再实践这样一个非线性的过程，它带给我的是对文学翻译本质的思考，对翻译艺术掌控力的把握，对文学翻译的全面观照。据我所知，微型小说译者的文化背景比较复杂，创作态度也良莠不齐，老一辈翻译家在语言文化基础和创作态度上是无可厚非的，基本表现为“全译”，可惜在文字上与原文“靠得太近”，人数也太少；中青年译者的数量居多，但语言文化基础大多不如前辈，在对原文的处理上“尺度过大”，多数表现为“编译”。

我生性保守，为人为文拘谨，记得曾经在《世界华文微型小说作家微自传》中这样总结过，“回首往事，也算是‘张三中’吧：‘心中’的原文，‘眼中’的译文，‘意中’的师生”。换句话说，对原文的敬畏，对译文的时代化，对青年、妇女儿童读者的念念不忘，千方百计地贴近时代，可能因此造就我的译文忠实性和可读性较强，基本表现为“全译”。

陈：果然如此，在您的译作中，我发现有几个题材是您情有独钟的，比如，青年、妇女和儿童，也就是说这是您自觉的文学追求，是您的“主观倾向”吧？

张：您一语中的。是的，身为女性，我“含泪的微笑”更多地落在了相似群体身上，是希望通过译作擦亮人文关怀的“镜与灯”。

陈：如果让您用几个关键词来概括您的翻译风格的话，您会选择哪些词？

张：首先进入我脑海的是：简洁、幽默、时尚。

陈：为什么是这三个词，而不是其他？

张：这个嘛，都缘于我的“本色演出”，我人简单直接，译文也就长不了；身为教书匠，我喜欢寓教于乐，译文也就搞文字狂欢；我的目标读者是青年，我的译文就各种“潮”，“一大波流行词语正在靠近”。

陈：嗯嗯，听出来啦。

最后，我还是要不客气地指出您在创作趋势上的一个问题，您的微型小说翻译在初期量大质优，“凡有井水处，皆能歌柳词”。而在近期却在数量上大不如前了，希望您可以有所弥补。

张：谢谢陈老师指教，我也意识到了这个问题。原因是多方面的，最重要的还是我目前的长篇著译、教学和研究生辅导让我分身乏术，不过，我一定竭尽心力，在理论上继续为微型小说翻译“鼓与呼”，在实践上做“颜色不一样的烟火”。

（本篇原载于中国作家网2015年9月9日 http://www.chinawriter.com.cn）

目 录

content

怎样成为百万富翁

［加拿大］斯蒂芬·里柯克

我经常和百万富翁们打交道。我喜欢他们。我喜欢他们的脸。我喜欢他们的生活方式。我喜欢他们吃的食物。和他们打交道越多，我就越喜欢他们的一切。

我尤其喜欢的是他们的衣着，他们灰色的格子裤、白色的格子背心、沉甸甸的金链子，以及他们用来签署支票的印章戒指。呀！他们看起来神气活现的。要是能看到他们六七个人一起坐在俱乐部里，不失为一种享受。他们的身上哪怕是沾上一丁点儿灰尘，都会有人跑去为他们掸掉。真的，而且很乐意这样。连我都乐意亲手为他们掸掉点儿灰尘。

我喜欢他们的饮食，但是我更喜欢他们学富五车。那真是了不起。看看他们看的书就一目了然了。他们简直就是手不释卷。无论何时到俱乐部去，你都会发现有三四个百万富翁在那里。看看他们读的那些东西吧！你准会认为，一个从上午11点到下午三点都在办公室努力工作、中间只有一个半小时吃中饭的人，一定会筋疲力尽。其实一点儿也不。这些人工作之余，照样能坐下来读《小品文》、《警察报》和《桃色苑》之类，而且跟我一样对其中的笑话心领神会。

我热衷于做的一件事是在他们中间走来走去，这样就可以捕捉到他们的只言片语了。几天前我听到其中一个百万富翁往前探着身体说："算了，我说了给他一百五十万，再多一分都不给，他要么拿走要么走人——"我多渴望能插上一句："什么！一百五十万哦！再说一遍！给我好了，要么拿走要么走人。一定给我这次机会啊，要么拿走要么走人，我知道我能马上答复您。只给一百万也行，我们一言为定。"

并不是说他们这些人对钱无所谓。不，先生，别那么想。他们对大笔大笔的钱当然是不太在乎的，比如说一出手便是十万八万的。但对小钱可不一样。除非你了解他们为了一分一厘，甚至不到一分一厘会急成什么样。

嘿，几天前的一个晚上，两个百万富翁欣喜若狂地进了俱乐部。他们说小麦涨价了，他们俩不到半个小时就各自赚了四分钱。这赚头让他们胃口大开，所以点了足够 16 个人吃的晚宴。我为报刊写稿挣到的钱是这点儿赚头的两倍，我都没这么炫耀过。

有一天晚上，我听见一个百万富翁说："喂，咱们打个电话给纽约，给他们两分五厘钱。"天哪！想想看，大半夜给人口近五百万的纽约城打电话，就为了给他们两分五厘钱，电话费还得多少钱呢？那么——是不是就此惹恼了纽约人呢？没有，他们接受了。当然，这是高级金融问题。我不想不懂装懂。此后我试着打电话到芝加哥，说给它一分五厘钱，另外我还打电话到安大略省的汉密尔顿，说给它五毛钱，但是接线员却以为我疯了。

当然，这一切都显示出我一直在研究百万富翁们成功的奥秘。我在做研究，已经研究很多年了。我认为对刚刚开始工作就想辞职不干的年轻人来说，这种研究可能还是很有帮助的。

你知道，很多人在生命中很晚的时期才意识到：如果他还是个孩子的时候他就明白了现在明白的事理，那么，他的人生就会大有作为。

而反过来，又有多少年轻人却没有进一步思考：假如他当年明白了他现在所不了解的那些东西，那他会有怎样的作为，又不会有怎样的作为呢？这些想法细思极恐。

总之，我一直在探寻百万富翁们的成功奥秘。

有一点我可以非常肯定：假如一个年轻人想成为百万富翁，那么必须对他的饮食和起居倍加小心。看来要做到这一点不容易。但是没有人能够随随便便成功，努力是唯一的途径。

一个想成为百万富翁的年轻人，却以为理所当然应该在七点半起床，早饭吃强力牌肉食和荷包蛋，午餐喝凉水，而且十点钟准时睡觉，那是不合适的。你不可以这么做。我见过太多的百万富翁，没见过这么做的。如果你想成为百万富翁，十点之前你不能起床。百万富翁们绝不这么做。他们不敢这么做。假如有人看见他们早上九点半就在街上，那他们的生意也就贬值了。

节俭的老观念根本就是错误的。要想成为百万富翁，你需要喝香槟酒，喝大量的香槟酒，一刻不停地喝。除了香槟，你还需要喝苏格兰威士忌和苏打水。你得几乎整个晚上都泡在这些酒里，成桶成桶地喝。酒能使你头脑清醒，头脑清醒第二天才能做生意。我见过一些这样的百万富翁，他们在早上头脑是那么清醒，红彤彤的脸确实像煮过一样。当然，像这样生活需要决心。不过你可以一品脱一品脱地买酒。

因此，我亲爱的年轻人，假如你想在生意方面更上一层楼，那就得改变一下生活方式。要是房东大娘给你端来熏肉和蛋作早餐，把它们扔到窗外去喂狗好了，叫她给你弄点儿凉拌芦笋和一品脱葡萄酒来。然后打个电话给你的老板，告诉他你大约十一点钟才会到。这样你就飞黄腾达起来。对，很快就会一步登天。

至于百万富翁们是怎样赚到一百万的，这个问题不好回答。但有一种办法是这样的：带五分钱进城打拼。百万富翁们几乎都是这样开始创业的。他们反反复复地告诉我（都是身价百万或千万的人），他们当初进城的时候身上只有五分钱。看来他们就是靠这点儿本钱开始创业的。当然，这困难重重。有一次我也差点儿这样发起来了。我当时借了五分钱，带着它出了城，后来就心急火燎地转身回了城，因为我如果没在郊外正好碰到一家啤酒馆，把那五分钱给花了的话，我今天可能已经是百万富翁了。

另一个上佳计划是创业。规模要大，要敢为天下先。比如说，有一个我认识的百万富翁告诉我说，想当年他在墨西哥，身无分文（他在中美洲把那五分钱的本钱亏掉了）。他却独具慧眼发现那里没有发电厂，于是他就创办了一个，结果赚了个盆满钵满。我认识的另一个百万富翁也差不多，他在纽约滞留时也是一文不名。不过，他突然灵机一动，想到纽约城需要盖一些比现有的高楼高十层的楼房。于是他就盖了两座，随即一售而空。很多百万富翁都是用这种简单的方法一夜暴富的。

当然，还有一种方法比上述任何一种方法还要容易。我几乎都舍不得把它说出来，因为我想留给自己。

我是有天晚上在俱乐部偶然听说的。俱乐部里有一个老先生，他富可敌国，那张脸就像最出色的鬣狗。我以前从不知道他是怎么成为百万富翁的。因此有一天晚上，我向一个百万富翁打听了一下布洛格斯这老家伙是怎样发家致富的。

“他怎么发的？”他轻蔑地回答说。“哎呀，他是在孤儿寡母身上发的财。”

孤儿寡母！妈呀，这个生意可真是奇思妙想！谁能想到孤儿和寡妇身上会有财可发呢？

“可是怎么操作呢？”我极其小心翼翼地问道。“他从他们身上直接抢？”

“哎呀，”那人回答说，“他只需把他们放在脚跟下面狠榨就行了，就这么回事儿。”

那么，是不是很简单啊？自那以后，我经常琢磨这次谈话，很想试一试。要是我能抓着他们，我会很快地榨干他们。可怎么才能把他们抓住呢？我所认识的寡妇大多数是那种很壮实的。至于孤儿，一定要数量众多才够。与此同时我还在等待时机，要是我能弄来一大批孤儿，我要踩在他们身上榨榨看。

通过求教，我还发现从牧师身上也可以榨出钱来。他们都说牧师们挺好榨的。不过，或许还是孤儿更容易榨些。

How to Make a Million Dollars

By Stephen Leacock

I mix a good deal with the Millionaires. I like them. I like their faces. I like the way they live. I like the things they eat. The more we mix together the better I like the things we mix.

Especially I like the way they dress, their grey check trousers, their white check waist-coats, their heavy gold chains, and the signet-rings that they sign their cheques with. Oh! They look nice. Get six or seven of them sitting together in the club and it's a treat to see them. And if they get the least dust on them, men come and brush it off. Yes, and are glad to. I'd like to take some of the dust off them myself.

Even more than what they eat I like their intellectual grasp. It is wonderful. Just watch them read. They simply read all the time. Go into the club at any hour and you'll see three or four of them at it. And the things they can read! You'd think that a man who'd been driving hard in the office from eleven o'clock until three, with only an hour and a half for lunch, would be too fagged. Not a bit. These men can sit down after office hours and read the Sketch and the Police Gazette and the Pink Un, and understand the jokes just as well as I can.

What I love to do is to walk up and down among them and catch the little scraps of conversation. The other day I heard one lean forward and say, "Well, I offered him a million and a half and said I wouldn't give a cent more, he could either take it or leave it—" I just longed to break in and say, "What! what! a million and a half! Oh! Say that again! Offer it to me, to either take it or leave it. Do try me once. I know I can, or here, make it a plain million and let's call it done."

Not that these men are careless over money. No, sir. Don't think it. Of course they don't take much account of big money, a hundred thousand dollars at a shot or anything of that sort. But little money. You've no idea till you know them how anxious they get about a cent, or half a cent, or less.

Why, two of them came into the club the other night just frantic with delight: they said wheat had risen and they'd cleaned up four cents each in less than half an hour. They bought a dinner for sixteen on the strength of it. I don't understand it. I've often made twice as much as that writing for the papers and never felt like boasting about it.

One night I heard one man say, "Well, let's call up New York and offer them a quarter of a cent." Great heavens! Imagine paying the cost of calling up New York, nearly five million people, late at night and offering them a quarter of a cent! And yet—did New York get mad? No, they took it. Of course it's high finance. I don't pretend to understand it. I tried after that to call up Chicago and offer it a cent and a half, and to call up Hamilton, Ontario, and offer it half a dollar, and the operator only thought I was crazy.

All this shows, of course, that I've been studying how the millionaires do it. I have. For years. I thought it might be helpful to young men just beginning to work and anxious to stop.

You know, many a man realizes late in life that if when he was a boy he had known what he knows now, instead of being what he is he might be what he won't; but how few boys stop to think that if they knew what they don't know instead of being what they will be, they wouldn't be? These are awful thoughts.

At any rate, I've been gathering hints on how it is they do it.

One thing I'm sure about. If a young man wants to make a million dollars he's got to be mighty careful about his diet and his living. This may seem hard. But success is only achieved with pains.

There is no use in a young man who hopes to make a million dollars thinking he's entitled to get up at 7:30a.m., eat force and poached eggs, drink cold water at lunch, and go to bed at 10 p.m. You can't do it. I've seen too many millionaires for that. If you want to be a millionaire you mustn't get up till ten in the morning. They never do. They daren't. It would be as much as their business is worth if they were seen on the street at half-past nine.

And the old idea of abstemiousness is all wrong. To be a millionaire you need champagne, lots of it and all the time. That and Scotch whisky and soda: you have to sit up nearly all night and drink buckets of it. This is what clears the brain for business next day. I've seen some of these men with their brains so clear in the morning, that their faces look positively boiled. To live like this requires, of course, resolution. But you can buy that by the pint.

Therefore, my dear young man, if you want to get moved on from your present status in business, change your life. When your landlady brings your bacon and eggs for breakfast, throw them out of window to the dog and tell her to bring you some chilled asparagus and a pint of Moselle. Then telephone to your employer that you'll be down about eleven o'clock. You will get moved on. Yes, very quickly.

Just how the millionaires make the money is a difficult question. But one way is this. Strike the town with five cents in your pocket. They nearly all do this; they've told me again and again (men with millions and millions) that the first time they struck town they had only five cents. That seems to have given them their start. Of course, it's not easy to do. I've tried it several times. I nearly did it once. I borrowed five cents, carried it away out of town, and then turned and came back at the town with an awful rush. If I hadn't struck a beer saloon in the suburbs and spent the five cents I might have been rich today.

Another good plan is to start something. Something on a huge scale: something nobody ever thought of. For instance, one man I know told me that once he was down in Mexico without a cent (he'd lost his five in striking Central America) and he noticed that they had no power plants. So he started some and made a mint of money. Another man that I know was once stranded in New York, absolutely without a nickel. Well, it occurred to him that what was needed were buildings ten stories higher than any that had been put up. So he built two and sold them right away. Ever so many millionaires begin in some such simple way as that.

There is, of course, a much easier way than any of these. I almost hate to tell this, because I want to do it myself.

I learned of it just by chance one night at the club. There is one old man there, extremely rich, with one of the best faces of the lot, just like a hyena. I never used to know how he had got so rich. So one evening I asked one of the millionaires how old Bloggs had made all his money.

"How he made it?" He answered with a sneer. "Why he made it by taking it out of widows and orphans."

Widows and orphans! I thought, what an excellent idea. But who would have suspected that they had it?

"And how," I asked pretty cautiously, "did he go at it to get it out of them?"

"Why," the man answered, "he just ground them under his heels, that was how."

Now isn't that simple? I've thought of that conversation often since and I mean to try it. If I can get hold of them, I'll grind them quick enough. But how to get them. Most of the widows I know look pretty solid for that sort of thing, and as for orphans, it must take an awful lot of them. Meantime I am waiting, and if I ever get a large bunch of orphans all together, I'll stamp on them and see.

I find, too, on inquiry, that you can also grind it out of clergymen. They say they grind nicely. But perhaps orphans are easier.

客服热线

一个顾客新买的计算机出现了一点儿小问题。这是计算机制造商的销售服务热线与顾客之间的笔录。

"晚上好，这里是达蒙电脑公司客服热线，请问我有什么可以帮到您的吗？"

"嗯，我刚从你们公司新买了一台电脑，电脑出现了一个小麻烦。"

"看起来是什么问题？"

"我一直在高高兴兴地使用 Word 文档，突然打出来的字不见了。"

"我懂了，在打的字不见了之前你备份（backed up）了吗？"

"后退（译者注：原文 backed up 既有'备份'，也有'后退'的意思 ）？你的意思是倒车似的往后退？"

"不是，我的意思是说你打的字不见了之前有没有保存。"

"没保存。"

"哦，天哪，嗯，让我们看看能不能帮你找回来。你现在在屏幕上能看到什么？"

"什么也看不到。"

"一点儿东西也看不到？"

"看不到，一片空白。"

"你能看到桌面吗？"

“能，能看到。”

“我们试着点击屏幕上的Word文档小图标，把它重新打开。”

“我告诉你了，那里彻底一片空白，什么都没有。”

“可是你说能看到桌面吧？”

“能，我能看到。”

“你能看到桌面上有什么？”

“我的电脑、手机和一杯茶。”

“我懂了，原来你指的是那个桌面。那好，我们换个做法试试，你显示器的电源灯是亮的吧？”

“显示器是什么东西？”

“就是你面前电视似的屏幕，你电脑上有亮着的小红灯或者小绿灯吧？”

“没有。”

“那好，你看看显示器后面插没插电源线？”

“稍等，我摸摸后面，插了。”

“电源线的那头插进墙上的插座里了吗？”

“插了呀，我看起来有那么笨吗？”

“那好，那好，我只不过想全面检查一下。显示器后面的缆线与电脑主机插牢了吧？”

“我不知道，我够不着那里。”

“那好，不过，你跪在书桌上，起码可以看到是插牢了或者插了一半什么的吧？”

“稍等，我去取个手电筒来。”

“手电筒？”

“现在唯一的一丝光是窗外的月光。”

“你不能开灯吗？”

“不能，我们这里刚才停电了。”

“停……停电了？那好，我们的问题理清了，你电脑的包装箱、说明书和收据还在吧？”

“在，都在，我昨天刚买的电脑嘛。”

“好，那就好。你需要把所有东西都放回纸箱，尽可能地保持原样，然后带着收据送回商店。”

“哦，不，问题真的这么大？”

“对，恐怕问题确实这么大。”

“好的，我到了那里跟他们说什么呢？”

“嗯，要求退款，告诉他们你确实太笨，根本无法使用电脑。”

咔嗒。

Help Line

This is the transcript of a PC manufacturer's new sales help line in conversation with a customer who was having a spot of bother with a new computer.

"Good evening, this is Damon, how can we help you?"

"Well I am having a little trouble with this new PC your company sold me."

"What appears to be the problem?"

"I was working away quite happily in the Word programme, when the words I was writing suddenly disappeared."

"I see, had you backed the file up before this happened."

"Backed it up, you mean like reversing it?"

"No, I mean like did you save them before you lost them."

"No."

"Oh dear, well let's see if we can try to find them for you. What can you see on your screen now?"

"Nothing."

"Nothing at all?"

"No, it is completely blank."

"Can you even see your desktop?"

"Yes. I can see that."

"Well try clicking on the little symbol for the word file on the screen and open it again."

"I told you it is completely blank, there's nothing there."

"But you said you could see your desktop?"

"I can."

"What can you see on it?"

"My computer, the phone and a mug of tea?"

"Ah I see, that desktop, OK, let's try this another way. Does your monitor have the power light on?"

"What is the monitor?"

"The screen in front of you that looks like a TV. Are there any small red or green lights on your computer anywhere?"

"No."

"OK, is the power cable still plugged into the back of the PC?"

"Hang on, I'll reach over the back-yes it is."

"OK, is the other end plugged into the wall?"

"Yes it is, look I'm not that stupid?"

"OK, OK, I am just going through all the checks. Is the cable between the back of the screen and the rest of the computer plugged in securely?"

"I don't know, I can't reach round there."

"OK, but if you kneel on the desk can you at least see if it is plugged in securely and not only half in or something like that?"

"Can you hang on, I will have to get a torch."

"A torch?"

"Yes, the only light I have on is coming in through the window."

"Can't you turn the room light on?"

"No, we've just had a power cut."

"A power... a power cut? OK, we have got this sorted out now, do you still have the boxes, manuals and a receipt?"

"Yes, they are all here, I only bought it yesterday."

"Good, that's good. You need to put everything back in the box, exactly as it came and take it all back to the shop with the receipt."

"Oh no, is it really that bad?"

"Yes, I am afraid it is that bad."

"OK, what shall I tell them when I get there?"

"Well, ask for your money back. Just tell them that you really are too stupid to own a computer after all."

Click.

招聘启事：只招外星人

［美国］雪莉·李

窗口的标识上写着："招聘启事：只招外星人。"

我的天哪，我步履沉重地走在街上，走啊走，想找到一家愿意雇用人类的雇主。自从美国微软公司实行大型外部求才计划以来，已经过去了三个月，整整三个月，我都没见过这家公司的内部是什么样。

我做了一个深呼吸，看着冰冷的气从我的唇间渗出，扩散到芝加哥的空气中。如果我再找不到一份工作，明天该怎么过？

"嗨，看着点儿！"一个声音传入我的耳朵。

我眨了眨朦胧的双眼，发觉自己撞到了一个人身上。"对不起。"我对那个外星人道歉——我也吃不准他是从哪颗星球来的——然后往后退，将我的双手从他的蓝色肌肤的胸部拿开（这是因为他的外套敞开着）。"我不是……"

我突然打住，低头看着自己的指尖。"是颜料吗……？"

过了几秒，我才明白这是怎么回事，可等我恍然大悟之时，胸口紧绷绷的疼痛感也消失不见了。"我的天啊。"我抬头看着"蓝色颜料先生"说，"你是……你是一个人……对不对？"

他惊恐地沉下了脸，就像垂下一个窗帘，他推开我，匆匆离去。

我转过身，看着他穿过人群，心中大惊。这可怎么好？我想知道，难道他就没被人识破过吗？

我不知该怎样回答这些问题，但我知道，假如我不试试这个男人的好方法，我就再也没法养活自己这一大家子人了。

面试官是个人类与外星人的混血儿，但一件黑色大衣遮盖了她的身体，因而她与纯种人类的区别只是前额上的那些金色斑点。

“那么，”她面带微笑地看着我，露出一排完美无瑕的牙齿，“阿里马诺先生，请告诉我，你的家族史如何？”

“呃，我出生在芝加哥，是本地人。我母亲从森尼星球来到地球，那时她还只有几百岁。两千年之后，当我父亲因公出差从波朗姆星球来到地球，他和我母亲结了婚。几年后，他俩生下了我。”

面试官点了点头，指着我的一双橘红色的手说，“我看见，你母亲赋予了你森尼星人的灵活手指，”她说，“用来打字会很完美。你打字的速度是多少？”

我的心仿佛一下子冻结了，因为我不知道外星人一般的打字速度有多快。“一分钟九百个单词。”我顿了顿，决定这么回答。

“呃。对于森尼星人来说，这个速度听上去有点儿慢，不过……”她耸了耸肩，在她面前的拍纸簿上写了“900”，“你只继承了你母亲的50%血统，这可能也合情合理。”

她抬起头看着我，黑色的眼睛穿透了我的身体，仿佛是要将我淹没进一个黑色的深渊，“阿里马诺先生，”她说，“你被雇用了。明天可以开始上班吗？”

这份工作没有我想象的那么困难。只要我一直待在雷达下面，尽可能少地与同事交往，勤奋工作，我肯定能保住这份工作。

慢慢地，冬去春来，然后又进入了夏季，而在我还未察觉之前，由夏入冬，冬季又回来了。只不过，现在我的家人头上有片瓦遮风雨，腹中不再饥肠辘辘——今年我甚至还可以给尼基和约尔买份圣诞节礼物，也许还会去度个小假期。

“嗨。”我的老板走过来，跟我打招呼。他曾经告诉过我，他是洛图斯星球来的，那是个沙漠星球，所以他的皮肤才这么绿，这么粗糙。“你有没有把为‘七部’准备的运货计划表打印出来？”

“打出来了。”我伸出手，想从打印机上抓起那张计划表，但我的胳膊不够长，没够着。

老板咯咯笑出声。“别担心，”他一边说，一边向我伸出手，“我会拿到的。”

可是，当他抽回手时，胳膊肘擦过我的脸庞。对于他那种肌肤的刺痛的质感，让我受不了。

所以，我打了个喷嚏。

起初，老板什么也没说，只是用他洞悉人心的目光凝视着我。然后，他低头看了一眼自己的手臂。

我不明白他为什么有这样的举动，直到我垂下头，看见喷在他手臂上的鼻涕里的血。

“这是人的血迹，”老板对我说，“对吧？”

我保持沉默，于是我俩又一次陷入了沉默。

我浑身上下都在哆嗦，但我根本停不下来。我能听见自己的心在跳，一声比一声高，简直就要从胸腔里蹦出来，直到最后老板斜靠过来，低声对我说道：“你搞定……这个毛病，好吧？我俩的这次邂逅就当从没发生过。”

我忙不迭地点头，大气都不敢出。

“圣诞节快乐。”他说着，走开了。

Outsourced

By Shelly Li

The sign in the window says: "Offering Jobs to Non-Humans Only."

Oh my God, I think as I trudge along the street, walking and walking to find an employer that will hire a human. It's been three months since the big outsourcing plan was put in place at Microsoft, three months since I'd even seen the inside of a corporate building.

I let out a deep breath, watch the cold smoke seep from my lips and spread out into the Chicago air. What if I never find a job again?

"Hey, watch it!" A voice bleeds into my ear.

I blink to clear the haze out of my eyes and notice that I've run into someone. "Sorry," I say to the alien—I'm not sure what planet he's from—and move back from the inside of his coat, taking my hands off his blue-coloured chest. "I didn't..."

I stop all of a sudden and look down at the tips of my fingers. "Paint...?"

It takes a few seconds for the meaning of this to sink in for me, but when it finally does, I feel the tightening pain in my chest disappear. "Oh my God," I say, looking up at Mr. Blue Paint. "You're...you're a human...aren't you?"

A terrified scowl drops over his face like a curtain, and he pushes past me and hurries away.

I turn around and watch him as he moves through the people around him, amazed. How can this be? I wonder. Has no one caught him yet?

I don't know the answers to these questions, but what I do know is that if I don't give this man's idea a try, I will not be able to feed my family for much longer.

The interviewer is half-human, half-alien, but with a black overcoat covering her body, the only thing that differentiates her from a full human are the golden spots cast across her forehead.

"So," she says, smiling at me with a row of perfect teeth. "Tell me, Mr. Alimano, what is your family history?"

"Well, I was born here in Chicago. My mother emigrated to Earth from Sennia when she was just a few centuries old. When my father came to Earth on business from Polum a couple of millennia later, he and my mother were wed. They gave birth to me a few years later."

The interviewer nodded and pointed to my orange-red hands. "I can see that your mother has given you flexible Sennian fingers," she says. "Those will be perfect for typing. What's your speed?"

My heart freezes then, for I do not know the normal typing speed of an alien. "Nine hundred words a minute," I decide to say after a little pause.

"Hmm. That sounds a little low for a Sennian, but..." She shrugs and writes "900" down on the notepad in front of her. "You are only 50% of your mother. It's probably reasonable."

She looks up at me, her black eyes piercing into mine, drowning me in a dark abyss. "Mr. Alimano," she says. "You're hired. Can you start tomorrow?"

The job is not as hard as I thought it would be. As long as I keep under the radar, socialize at a minimum with my co-workers, and work hard, I am sure that I will stay employed.

Slowly, winter turns to spring, then fades into summer. Summer rolls into autumn, and before I know it, winter is here again. But now my family is living with a roof over their heads and food in their stomachs—perhaps I will even buy Christmas gifts for Nicky and Joel this year, or maybe take a little vacation.

"Hey," my boss walks up and says to me. He once told me that he was from Lotruus, the desert planet, which is why his skin is so green and tough. "Have you typed up the shipment schedule for Sector Seven yet?"

"Yes." I reach over and grab the schedule from the printer, but my arm does not extend far enough.

My boss chuckles. "Don't worry," he says, and reaches over me. "I'll grab it."

But his elbow rubs up against my face as he pulls back, and the tingly texture of his skin is too much for me to handle.

I sneeze.

For a moment, my boss says nothing, merely stares at me with those piercing eyes of his. Then he glances down at his arm.

I don't understand why he is acting this way until I look down and see the blood mixed in with the snot on his arm.

"This is the blood of a human," my boss says to me. "Isn't it?"

I keep quiet, and we lapse into silence yet again.

Shivers are rolling through my body, but I can do nothing to stop them. I can hear my heart pounding, louder and louder, almost threatening to burst out of my chest when finally, my boss leans in and whispers to me: "You fix this...ailment of yours, okay? This encounter of ours did not happen."

I nod, not even daring to breathe.

"Merry Christmas," he says, and walks away.

换　货

［英国］乔恩·兰福德

“你好，先生。我能为您效劳吗？”

“劳驾，我想把这个闹钟退了。”

“闹钟怎么了？”

“闹钟坏了。”

“你是什么意思？”

“闹铃不响了。”

“你按照使用手册上的说明检修了吗？”

“修了。”

“还不行？”

“不行。”

“好吧。你有收据吗？”

“没有，我到处找，没找着。”

“那我就不能退款了。”

“哦，不，你误会了。我不想退钱。我只想换个能用的。”

“好吧。你有原始包装吗？”

“没有，我把它扔掉了。”

“如果没有原始包装，我就不能换货。”

“买的时候就包了个塑料壳，我用刀子才能开。我不明白，你为什么要包装呢？”

“我们换货的规定是产品带原始包装返还。”

“那只是一堆破塑料。我留它干吗？”

“就为万一你需要退货。”

“我没承想几周后闹钟就会坏掉。你是说你也没办法了？”

“做什么都需要一些购买证据。”

“我就是证据！我现在告诉你，我就是在这里买的。事实上，我想就是你卖给我的。”

“你在网上注册了产品保修序列号吗？”

“没有。”

“啊，这就成问题了。你当时是怎么付的款？现金还是信用卡？”

“现金。”

“如果你用的是信用卡，你就可以得到银行的一份声明，证明你什么时间在这里买了东西。”

“嗯，我付的是现金。”

“问题是，其他商店也卖这个牌子，你也可能是在任何地方买的。”

“有这个可能，可我没有。我是在这里买的，闹钟不闹了，你欠我一个闹钟。”

“你什么时候买的？”

“几个星期前。”

“我们的兑换规定是二十一天，所以你可能过了保修期了。”

“我上个月买的。我不记得具体日期了。”

“这种型号的闹钟我们已经卖了好几年了。”

“你是说我在撒谎？”

“那倒不是，先生。我只是说你可能在22天前买的，那样的话，即使有收据和原始包装，我也爱莫能助了。”

“一点儿忙也帮不上？”

“帮不上。”

“那么，我现在的闹钟就永远这么坏着？”

“嗯，你可以把它发回原制造商，附加一封信说明情况。”

“这是中国制造的，寄过去比买个新的都麻烦。”

“那么我建议把它送到修理店去修。”

“修这类东西通常比买还贵。”

“我知道。”

“我能和经理谈谈吗？”

“经理今天休息。”

“那么，我能和负责的人通话吗？”

“我就是。”

“经理明天来吗？”

“不来。”

“他下次什么时候进来？”

“是女的她。”

“好吧。她什么时候进来？”

“下星期一。”

“那么我下星期一再来。”

“很好。先生，我今天还能帮你什么事吗？”

“我十分怀疑。”

“好吧。你要办一张本店会员卡吗？这是完全免费的，你每次买东西的时候都会打九五折。”

“不用了，谢谢你。”

“如果你今天办卡，你会得到一份免费礼物。”

“什么免费礼物？”

“一个闹钟。”

The Exchange

By Jon Langford

"Hello, sir. How may I help you?"

"I'd like to return this alarm clock, please."

"What's wrong with it?"

"The alarm doesn't work."

"How do you mean?"

"The alarm makes no sound."

"Did you troubleshoot using the manual?"

"Yes."

"And it still didn't work?"

"No."

"Okay. Do you have the receipt?"

"No. I can't find it anywhere."

"Then I can't give you a refund."

"Oh no, you misunderstand. I don't want a refund. I just want to exchange it for one that works."

"Okay. Do you have the original packaging?"

"No. I threw it away."

"I can't do an exchange without the original packaging."

"It came in a plastic clamshell. I had to hack it open with a knife. I don't understand. Why do you need the packaging?"

"Our policy for all exchanges is that the product be returned in its original packaging."

"It was just a load of ripped up plastic. Why would I keep that?"

"In case you needed to return the item."

"I didn't think an alarm clock would break after a few weeks. So you're telling me you can't do anything to help?"

"To do anything I need some proof of purchase."

"I'm proof! I'm telling you now that I bought it here. In fact, I think you might have even served me."

"Did you register the product warranty number online?"

"No."

"Ah well, that's a problem. How did you pay for it? Cash or card?"

"Cash."

"If you'd paid on card you could've got a statement from your bank proving you'd made a purchase here and on what date."

"Well, I paid cash."

"The thing is, other stores sell this brand, too. You could've bought it anywhere."

"I could. But I didn't. I bought it here and it doesn't work and you owe me an alarm clock."

"When did you buy it?"

"A few weeks ago."

"Our exchange policy is twenty-one days so you might be out of warranty anyway."

"I bought it last month sometime. I don't remember the exact date."

"We've been selling this model for a couple of years now."

"Are you saying I'm lying?"

"No, sir. I'm simply saying that you might have bought it twenty-two days ago and in that case, even with a receipt and the original packaging, I wouldn't be able to do anything to help."

"Nothing?"

"No."

"So now I just have a faulty alarm clock forever?"

"Well, you could send it off to the manufacturer with a letter explaining the problem."

"It was made in China. That's more hassle than it's worth."

"Then I would suggest taking it to a repair shop."

"That sort of thing usually costs more than what you paid for something in the first place."

"I know."

"Can I speak to the manager, please?"

"The manager's off today."

"Then can I speak to whoever's in charge?"

"You already are."

"Is the manager in tomorrow?"

"No."

"When's he next in?"

"It's a she."

"Okay. When's she next in?"

"Monday."

"I'll come back Monday then."

"Very good. Can I help you with anything else today, sir?"

"I doubt it."

"Okay. Would you like to open a store card? It's completely free and you get five percent off every purchase."

"No thank you."

"If you open one today you get a free gift."

"What's the free gift?"

"An alarm clock."

借火柴

［加拿大］斯蒂芬·里柯克

你或许以为在大街上向人借根火柴易如反掌。但任何一个曾在街上向人借过火柴的人，都会向你保证没那么容易，而且在听了我那天傍晚的经历之后，他们还会赌咒发誓地说我所讲的事儿真而又真。

那天傍晚我站在一条街的拐角，手里拿着一支雪茄想点着，可是身上没带火柴。我便在那儿等着，直到有一个衣着体面、相貌平平的男人走了过来。于是我说：

“不好意思，先生，您可以借根火柴给我吗？”

“一根火柴？”他说。“哦，当然可以。”然后他解开大衣的扣子，把手伸进马甲口袋里摸了起来。“我记得我是有一根来着，”他继续摸索，“而且我几乎可以发誓它就在屁股后面的口袋里——哦，等等，话虽这么说，但我想也有可能是在上衣口袋里——请等一等，等我把这些包裹先放到人行道上。”

“哦，不用麻烦了，”我说，“这不重要。”

“哦，一点儿也不麻烦，我一会儿就找出来了。我记得我这里是有一根的，在哪个地方的。”——他一边说一边把手指伸进一个又一个口袋——“可是，你瞧，这不是我平时穿的那件马甲……”

我发现那个男人激动起来了。“好了，没什么的，”我反对说，“既然不是你平时常穿的那件马甲——嗨，那就没关系了。”

“等一等，喂，等一等！”那个男人说，“我身上的某个地方是有那么一根该死的东西的。我猜一定是和我的表放在一起。不对呀，也不在这儿。等一等，我再看看大衣里。要是那个讨厌的裁缝懂得口袋应该可以伸进手去就好啦！”

现在他变得更加激动了。他已扔掉手杖，正在咬牙切齿地摸索一个个口袋。“一定是我那该死的小儿子干的好事儿，”他怒气冲冲地低声说道，“都怪他在我口袋里乱掏。我对天发誓！回去我一定给他个教训！我说，我敢打赌，它是放在我的屁股口袋里。请你帮我把大衣的尾部提起来一会儿，等我……”

“不用了，不用了，”我再一次反对道，“请不要这么大费周章，真的不重要的。我觉得你没有必要脱掉大衣，哦，请不要把你的信件和东西扔在雪地里，也不要把你的口袋全部翻个底儿朝天！请你，请你不要踩在你的大衣上，也不要在那些小包中间踩来踩去。你用那种特别的、怨气冲天的声音咒骂你的小儿子，我听不下去。不要这样——请不要再撕扯你的衣服了。”

突然那汉子发出一阵狂喜的咕哝声，然后把他的手从大衣的衬里中抽了出来。

“我找到了。”他叫道。“给你！”然后他把它拿到了灯光下。

原来是一根牙签！

我按捺不住，冲动之下，一把将他推倒在电车轮下，转身逃之夭夭。

Borrowing a Match

By Stephen Leacock

You might think that borrowing a match upon the street is a simple thing. But any man who has ever tried it will assure you that it is not, and will be prepared to swear to the truth of my experience of the other evening.

I was standing on the corner of the street with a cigar that I wanted to light. I had no match. I waited till a decent, ordinary-looking man came along. Then I said:

"Excuse me, sir, but could you oblige me with the loan of a match?"

"A match?" he said, "why certainly." Then he unbuttoned his overcoat and put his hand in the pocket of his waistcoat. "I know I have one," he went on, "and I'd almost swear it's in the bottom pocket—or, hold on, though, I guess it may be in the top—just wait till I put these parcels down on the sidewalk."

"Oh, don't trouble," I said, "it's really of no consequence."

"Oh, it's no trouble, I'll have it in a minute; I know there must be one in here somewhere" —he was digging his fingers into his pockets as he spoke— "but you see this isn't the waistcoat I generally..."

I saw that the man was getting excited about it. "Well, never mind," I protested; "if that isn't the waistcoat that you generally—why, it doesn't matter."

"Hold on, now, hold on!" the man said, "I've got one of the cursed things in here somewhere. I guess it must be in with my watch. No, it's not there, either. Wait till I try my coat. If that confounded tailor only knew enough to make a pocket so that a man could get at it!"

He was getting pretty well worked up now. He had thrown down his walking-stick and was plunging at his pockets with his teeth set. "It's that cursed young boy of mine," he hissed; "this comes of his fooling in my pockets. By Gad! perhaps I won't warm him up when I get home. Say, I'll bet that it's in my hip-pocket. You just hold up the tail of my overcoat a second till I..."

"No, no," I protested again, "please don't take all this trouble, it really doesn't matter. I'm sure you needn't take off your overcoat, and oh, pray don't throw away your letters and things in the snow like that, and tear out your pockets by the roots! Please, please don't trample over your overcoat and put your feet through the parcels. I do hate to hear you swearing at your little boy, with that peculiar whine in your voice. Don't—please don't tear your clothes so savagely."

Suddenly the man gave a grunt of exultation, and drew his hand up from inside the lining of his coat.

"I've got it," he cried. "Here you are!" Then he brought it out under the light.

It was a toothpick.

Yielding to the impulse of the moment I pushed him under the wheels of a trolley-car, and ran.

拼字游戏导致的死亡

［美国］查理·菲什

天气炎热，我恨我太太。

我们在玩拼字游戏。就是这么糟糕，今年42岁的我，在这么个烈日炎炎的周日下午，我能想到的生活里唯一可行的就是玩拼字游戏。

我本应出外锻炼锻炼身体，花花钱，接触接触人，从周四早晨开始到现在，除了我太太，我都没跟别人说过话。对，周四早晨我跟送牛奶的人确实说过话。

我的字母牌很烂。

我十分应景地拼了“开始”（BEGIN），字母N在小小的粉格子上。22分。

我看着我太太重新排列组合字母时那洋洋得意的表情，听着那噼噼啪啪的声音，我恨她。倘若没有她在身边的话，我此刻会做一些有趣的事：我会攀登乞力马扎罗山，我会在好莱坞最新大片里领衔主演，我会驾驶一艘名为“新视野”的60英尺的快速帆船，在温妮环球赛上大显身手——我不知道到底会做什么，可我一定会做点儿什么的。

她拼了“倒霉的”（JINXED），字母J在双倍分字母格，30分。她已经开始动手打我了，也许我应该宰了她才对。

倘若我有一个D字母就好了，那样的话，我就可以拼“杀手”（MURDER）这个词了，那会是一声叹息，那会是一张许可证。

我从袋子里拿新字母的时候，发现自己在想——这个字母会告诉我下一步该做什么。倘若拼出的是“宰杀”，或者“刺杀”，或者是她的名字，或者别的什么，我都会立刻动手，把她干掉。

我的那排拼出的是“MIHZPA”，再加上我嘴里的U，该死的。

烈日透过窗户烤在我身上。我能听到窗外昆虫的嗡嗡声，我希望外面不是蜜蜂，因为我的表弟哈罗德九岁的时候吞进了一只蜜蜂，然后喉咙肿胀，最后死了。如果外面是蜜蜂，我希望它们飞进我太太的喉咙。

她拼出了“流汗”（SWEATIER），动用了她的全部字母，得了24分，外加50分奖励分。倘若不是天气太热我懒得动的话，我现在就勒死她。

我的汗流得更厉害了，需要雨水来清新空气。这个念头在我的脑海里刚刚闪过，我就找到另一个好词。使用JINXED里的D字母，“湿润的 ”（HUMID）得了两个词的分。我把U字母放下的时候，有点儿唾液飞溅。又一个22分。我希望她还有大量的字母牌。

她告诉我她有大量的字母牌。由于某种原因，我更恨她了。

她拼了“狂热者”（FAN），F字母在双倍积分格上。她起身灌了壶水，打开了空调。

这是十年来最热的一年，我太太却烧起了水，所以我恨我太太。我拼了“枪杀”（ZAPS），Z字母在双倍积分上。她把空调调到了静音模式，对此，我心满意足。

她长叹一声，回来坐下，又重新开始摆弄她的字母牌，噼噼啪啪。我感到怒火中烧，一种内心的毒素在四肢蔓延开来，快要抵达指尖时，我就要从椅子上一跃而起，一把将拼字盘掀翻到地板上，开始一次又一次地揍她。

愤怒到了我的指尖却过去了，我心跳如捣，我浑身大汗淋漓，我想其实我的脸色也变了。然后，我长叹一声，坐回椅子里。水壶开始响起了哨音，它越吹我越热。

她在双倍积分格子上拼了“准备好了”（READY），得了18分。然后给自己泡了杯热茶。不，我不想喝。

我趁她不备，从字母袋里偷了一张孤张牌，从我的盘里拿出一张V字母牌丢进字母袋。她狐疑地看了我一眼。她端着她那杯茶走了回来坐下，在桌子上放了一个优胜杯，而我拼了一个八个字母的单词：“作弊”（CHEATING），还用了“准备”（READY）里的A字母。得了64分，包括50分的奖励分，这说明我现在占了她的上风。

她问我是不是作弊了。

我真是恨她，恨死她了。

她拼了三倍积分词“视而不见”（IGNORE），得了21分。现在她153分，我155分。

她茶杯上热气蒸腾，让我更觉燥热。我想在我的盘上拼个与谋杀有关的词，可我能拼得最好的词是“睡觉”（SLEEP）。

我太太一直处于嗜睡状态。我们邻居大吵大闹，最后把门都踹破，电视机都砸了，天线宝宝都掏空了，而她全程都在睡觉，第二天还因为缺觉跟我闹情绪，埋怨我。

要是有办法除掉她该有多好。

我瞅准了一个机会，动用我所有的字母，用了“倒霉”（JINXED）里的X字母，得了72分。给她个下马威。

我放下最后一个字母的时候，只听一声震耳欲聋的巨响，空调坏了。

我的心跳加速，不是被那声巨响吓的。我不信——可这不可能是一个巧合。是这些字母的力量。我拼了“爆炸”（EXPLODES）这个词，就真爆炸了——空调爆炸了。此前，我作弊以后拼了“作弊”（CHEATING）这个词。我拼了“击中”（ZAP）以后，我太太就触电了。这些词都变成了现实。这些字母都在选择它们的未来。整个游戏就是——“倒霉”（JINXED）。

我太太在三倍积分格上拼了“叹息”（SIGN），得了 10 分。

我要检验一下。

我得拼点儿什么，看能否变成现实。拼点儿不大可能发生的，来证明是字母的力量。我盘上有 ABQYFWE，给我留下的选择余地不大，我开始疯狂地咬 B 字母。

我拼了“飞翔”（FLY），用了“爆炸”（EXPLODES）里的 L。我靠回椅背上，合上双眼，等待从椅子上腾空而起的感觉，等待飞翔。

愚蠢。我睁开了眼睛，有一只会飞的苍蝇。一个昆虫，在拼字盘上盘旋，在温热的茶杯冒出的热气里冲浪。这什么都证明不了，苍蝇原来就在那里。

我需要拼一个准确无误的词，一个不会被误会的词，一个绝对的、终极的词，一个一了百了的词，一个关于谋杀的词。

我太太拼了“小心”（CAUTION），用一张孤张牌代替 N 字母，得了 18 分。

我的盘里有 AQWEUK，加上我嘴里的字母 B。我对字母的力量心存敬畏，也为不能支配这种力量而沮丧。也许我应该再作一次弊，抽出一些字母组成“砍”（SLASH）或者“杀”（SLAY）。

这让我灵机一动。这个完美的词，一个集力量、危险、恐惧于一身的词。

我拼了“震动”（QUAKE）一词，得了 19 分。

我不知道震动的力量与所得的分数是否匹配。我能感受到静脉里那股潜在的颤抖之力。我在掌控命运。我在操纵命运。

我太太拼了“死亡”（DEATH）一词，得了 34 分，就在房间开始震动的时候。

我大吃一惊，喘着气为自己辩解——我咬着的 B 字母卡在我喉咙里了。我试着咳嗽。我的脸变红了，然后变蓝了。我喉咙肿了。我抓喉咙抓出了血。地震达到了高潮。

我倒在了地上。我太太坐在那里纹丝不动，袖手旁观。

Death by Scrabble

By Charlie Fish

It's a hot day and I hate my wife.

We're playing Scrabble. That's how bad it is. I'm 42 years old, it's a blistering hot Sunday afternoon and all I can think of to do with my life is to play Scrabble.

I should be out, doing exercise, spending money, meeting people. I don't think I've spoken to anyone except my wife since Thursday morning. On Thursday morning I spoke to the milkman.

My letters are crap.

I play, appropriately, BEGIN. With the N on the little pink star. Twenty-two points.

I watch my wife's smug expression as she rearranges her letters. Clack, clack, clack. I hate her. If she wasn't around, I'd be doing something interesting right now. I'd be climbing Mount Kilimanjaro. I'd be starring in the latest Hollywood blockbuster. I'd be sailing the Vendee Globe on a 60-foot clipper called the New Horizons—I don't know, but I'd be doing something.

She plays JINXED, with the J on a double-letter score. 30 points. She's beating me already. Maybe I should kill her.

If only I had a D, then I could play MURDER. That would be a sign. That would be permission.

As I'm picking new letters from the bag, I find myself thinking—the letters will tell me what to do. If they spell out KILL, or STAB, or her name, or anything, I'll do it right now. I'll finish her off.

My rack spells MIHZPA. Plus the U in my mouth. Damn.

The heat of the sun is pushing at me through the window. I can hear buzzing insects outside. I hope they're not bees. My cousin Harold swallowed a bee when he was nine, his throat swelled up and he died. I hope that if they are bees, they fly into my wife's throat.

She plays SWEATIER, using all her letters. 24 points plus a 50 point bonus. If it wasn't too hot to move I would strangle her right now.

I am getting sweatier. It needs to rain, to clear the air. As soon as that thought crosses my mind, I find a good word. HUMID on a double-word score, using the D of JINXED. The U makes a little splash of saliva when I put it down. Another 22 points. I hope she has lousy letters.

She tells me she has lousy letters. For some reason, I hate her more.

She plays FAN, with the F on a double-letter, and gets up to fill the kettle and turn on the air conditioning.

It's the hottest day for ten years and my wife is turning on the kettle. This is why I hate my wife. I play ZAPS, with the Z doubled, and she gets a static shock off the air conditioning unit. I find this remarkably satisfying.

She sits back down with a heavy sigh and starts fiddling with her letters again. Clack clack. Clack clack. I feel a terrible rage build up inside me. Some inner poison slowly spreading through my limbs, and when it gets to my fingertips I am going to jump out of my chair, spilling the Scrabble tiles over the floor, and I am going to start hitting her again and again and again.

The rage gets to my fingertips and passes. My heart is beating. I'm sweating. I think my face actually twitches. Then I sigh, deeply, and sit back into my chair. The kettle starts whistling. As the whistle builds it makes me feel hotter.

She plays READY on a double-word for 18 points, then goes to pour herself a cup of tea. No I do not want one.

I steal a blank tile from the letter bag when she's not looking, and throw back a V from my rack. She gives me a suspicious look. She sits back down with her cup of tea, making a cup-ring on the table, as I play an 8-letter word: CHEATING, using the A of READY. 64 points, including the 50-point bonus, which means I'm beating her now.

She asks me if I cheated.

I really, really hate her.

She plays IGNORE on the triple-word for 21 points. The score is 153 to her, 155 to me.

The steam rising from her cup of tea makes me feel hotter. I try to make murderous words with the letters on my rack, but the best I can do is SLEEP.

My wife sleeps all the time. She slept through an argument our next-door neighbours had that resulted in a broken door, a smashed TV and a Teletubby Lala doll with all the stuffing coming out. And then she bitched at me for being moody the next day from lack of sleep.

If only there was some way for me to get rid of her.

I spot a chance to use all my letters. EXPLODES, using the X of JINXED. 72 points. That'll show her.

As I put the last letter down, there is a deafening bang and the air conditioning unit fails.

My heart is racing, but not from the shock of the bang. I don't believe it—but it can't be a coincidence. The letters made it happen. I played the word EXPLODES, and it happened—the air conditioning unit exploded. And before, I played the word CHEATING when I cheated. And ZAP when my wife got the electric shock. The words are coming true. The letters are choosing their future. The whole game is—JINXED.

My wife plays SIGN, with the N on a triple-letter, for 10 points.

I have to test this.

I have to play something and see if it happens. Something unlikely, to prove that the letters are making it happen. My rack is ABQYFWE. That doesn't leave me with a lot of options. I start frantically chewing on the B.

I play FLY, using the L of EXPLODES. I sit back in my chair and close my eyes, waiting for the sensation of rising up from my chair. Waiting to fly.

Stupid. I open my eyes, and there's a fly. An insect, buzzing around above the Scrabble board, surfing the thermals from the tepid cup of tea. That proves nothing. The fly could have been there anyway.

I need to play something unambiguous. Something that cannot be misinterpreted. Something absolute and final. Something terminal. Something murderous.

My wife plays CAUTION, using a blank tile for the N. 18 points.

My rack is AQWEUK, plus the B in my mouth. I am awed by the power of the letters, and frustrated that I cannot wield it. Maybe I should cheat again, and pick out the letters I need to spell SLASH or SLAY.

Then it hits me. The perfect word. A powerful, dangerous,

terrible word.

I play QUAKE for 19 points.

I wonder if the strength of the quake will be proportionate to how many points it scored. I can feel the trembling energy of potential in my veins. I am commanding fate. I am manipulating destiny.

My wife plays DEATH for 34 points, just as the room starts to shake.

I gasp with surprise and vindication—and the B that I was chewing on gets lodged in my throat. I try to cough. My face goes red, then blue. My throat swells. I draw blood clawing at my neck. The earthquake builds to a climax.

I fall to the floor. My wife just sits there, watching.

许可证

［阿富汗］巴希尔·萨哈瓦兹

你去快速冲个澡，但是花一万年时间刮你那永远刮不平的脸。你穿上白色的尼赫鲁牌衬衫和保罗·史密斯牌裤子，然后走进客厅，疯狂地寻找。“那破玩意儿在哪儿？”你大声喊道。你的妻子和女儿——全家——都开始帮你找。它不在通常所放的地方——不在客厅里杂乱无章的架子间，也不在卧室里半整洁的架子上。它不在厨房里。它不在任何一件上衣的口袋里。它在那里：在沙发的垫子下面。是你十几岁的女儿发现的。是你昨晚放的，你个白痴！这些天，你不再为自己经常犯的错误感到难为情，认为人老是你继续犯错误的许可证。你把许可证藏在你的皮肤下，让所有人都能看到你满是皱纹的脸。

你用这破玩意儿打开了汽车找到卫星导航。回到客厅，你的天才女儿，没有老年许可证的女儿，帮你把地址输入 GPS。输完后，你又大声喊了一声，准备好了吗？你妻子已经准备好了很长时间了，甚至在你开始找该死的它之前就准备好了。她拿着一个大塑料袋走了下来，你们俩都向女儿道别。

你不需要任何精巧的装置就能去洛桑。你知道路，所以在你进城之前不需要卫星导航。你不喜欢一个没有身体的女人尖叫着要你左转或右转的破坏性声音。在车里，你妻子和埃里克·克拉普顿在一起，而你和索菲在一起。每个人都说索菲的故事是一本潜在的畅销书，只要你能最终找到一个转折点。你的思绪艰难地走到罗盘的各个点上，但那股扭曲的思绪仍然无法避开你。突然间，就像你早在爱因斯坦之前就发现了相对论一样，你在脑海里大声喊，以免打扰到你妻子纳吉斯和埃里克在一起的亲密时刻：是的，是的，是的，它起作用了！索菲遇到了格雷格，她的第一个男朋友，她真正的爱人，她背着背包去泰国，在和西蒙结婚前一周就从生活中消失了。格雷格不知从哪儿冒出来，把她弄糊涂了。索菲完蛋了，但你的畅销书有点儿扭曲。

奇怪的事情发生在这个世界上。牛顿在一棵苹果树下发现了重力，小乔尼在衣柜里玩捉迷藏时，他发现他的母亲跟理查德叔叔在一起，你在开车去洛桑的时候现了索菲故事的扭曲。

你毫无意外地到达了这个城市。燃油箱仍然处于健康状态，你注意到了高速摄像头，没有人向你伸出两个手指来抱怨你的糟糕驾驶，纳吉斯也没有絮叨你是个没用的丈夫。

现在是使用它的时候了——但它不在那里！你把这些东西忘在起居室了。你开始诅咒自己。你这个白痴，你连最简单的任务都处理不了，比如到达目的地。你不得不回去，因为那该死的地址在那破玩意儿里。你的妻子加上了她自己的诅咒，但却显示了她的智慧。她打电话回家告诉你女儿你忘记了卫星导航系统。你的女儿——你的无薪秘书——准备再次帮你脱离困境。你妻子把电话放在扬声器上。

“是的，爸爸，左转进入格兰西大街。”

“你确定吗？”

“谷歌地图上就是这么写的。”

“但卫星导航系统不是这样的。”

纳吉斯失去了耐心，告诉你闭嘴，听你女儿的话。过了学校以后你错过了转弯，在到达U形转弯之前你必须开很长一段路。你向过路人问路，最后——完毕——你到达詹姆斯的家，迟到了整整一个小时。你按一下门铃：没人接。你再按一下门铃，以为詹姆斯一定在忙着招待其他客人。按了第三次以后，詹姆斯出现在门口。

“嗨，詹姆斯，生日快乐！”

“什么？”詹姆斯惊讶地说。

“今天是你的生……”

“下周是！”

“在我的日记里写的是今天。”

“不，下星期三才是。你一定把页数写错了。”

“不是……呃……今天？”

你看着纳吉斯，她的眼睛充满了愤怒和失望。她身上穿着她最好的衣服。

Licence

By Bashir Sakhawarz

You go for a quick shower but spend ages shaving your uneven face. You put on your white Nehru shirt with your Paul Smith trousers and go down to the living room, searching frantically. "Where's the shit?" you shout. Your wife and daughter—the whole family—start looking for it. It's not in its usual place-not amid the untidy overflow of the shelves in the living room, not on the semi-tidy shelves in the bedroom. It's not in the kitchen. It's not in any coat pocket. There it is: under a cushion on the sofa. It's your teenage daughter who finds it. That's where you put it last night, you idiot! These days you no longer feel embarrassed by your frequent mistakes, believing old age is your licence to carry on making blunders. You keep that licence under your skin, for all to see on your creased face.

You use the shit to open the car and find the satnav. Back in the living room, your genius daughter, who does not have the old-age licence, helps you to tap the address into the GPS. As soon as that's done you shout again, are you ready? Your wife has been ready for a long time, even before you started looking for the shit. She comes down with a large plastic bag and you both say goodbye to your daughter.

You head for Lausanne without needing any gadget. You know the way, so you won't need the satnav until you're inside the city. You don't like the disruptive sound of a disembodied woman's voice screeching at you to turn left or right. In the car your wife is with Eric Clapton and you're with Sofi. Everyone's saying that Sofi's story is a potential bestseller if only you can find a twist at the end. Your thoughts trek to all the points of the compass, but still that twist eludes you. Suddenly, as if you'd discovered the theory of relativity well before Einstein, you shout inside your head, so as not to disturb the intimate moments your wife Nargis is enjoying with Eric: yes, yes, yes, it works! Sofi bumps into Greg, her first boyfriend, her real love who went backpacking to Thailand and disappeared from her life, just one week before her marriage to Simon. Greg has surfaced from nowhere, throwing her into confusion. Sofi is screwed but there's the twist to your bestseller.

Strange things happen in this world. Newton discovered gravity under an apple tree, little Johnny was playing hide-and-seek in the wardrobe when he caught his mother with Uncle Richard, and you discovered the twist in Sofi's story while driving to Lausanne.

You reach the city without incident. The fuel tank is still in a healthy state, you were mindful of the speed cameras, nobody stuck two fingers up at you to complain of your bad driving, and Nargis didn't nag about you being a useless husband.

Now it's time to use it—but it's not there! You've left the shit in the living room. You start cursing yourself. You idiot, you can't even handle the simplest of tasks like reaching a destination. You'll have to turn back because the address is in that shit. Your wife adds curses of her own, but then displays her intelligence. She calls home and tells your daughter that you have forgotten the satnav. Your daughter—your unpaid secretary—is ready to bail you out yet again. Your wife puts the phone on speaker.

"Yes Dad, turn left into avenue Grancy."

"Are you sure?"

"That's what it says on Google maps."

"But it wasn't like that in the satnav."

Nargis loses her patience and tells you to shut up and listen to your daughter. You miss the turning after the school, and you have to drive a long way before reaching a U-turn. You ask a passerby for directions, and finally—bingo—you reach James's house, a whole hour late. You press the bell once: no answer. You press the bell again, thinking that James must be busy with his other guests. After the third ring, James appears at the door.

"Hi James, happy birthday!"

"What?" says James in surprise.

"It's your bir-bir-birth—"

"Next week!"

"It says today in my diary."

"No, next Wednesday. You must have put it on the wrong page."

"Not...er...today?"

You look at Nargis, her eyes are two oceans of anger and disappointment. She's wearing her best dress.

米尔博米纳斯·琼斯的悲惨命运

［加拿大］斯蒂芬·里柯克

有些人——当然，并非你我，因为我们都是非常有自制力的人——不过，确实有那么一些人，在与某人打电话时，或者傍晚造访别人家时，在需要告别离开的时候就会感到困难重重。时间越来越晚，到了那么一个时刻，客人终于觉得自己有权要求离开了，于是他突然站起身来，突然开口说道："好吧，我想我……"然后，主人说："哦，你现在非走不可吗？时间肯定还早呢！"紧接着客人心里又是一番可怜的挣扎。

我认为，在我所知道的这种事情中，经历最悲惨的就是我可怜的朋友米尔博米纳斯·琼斯了。他是一位助理牧师，一位可爱的年轻人，才23岁啊！他就是那种不会在主人面前脱身的人。他为人非常谦虚，不会撒谎，笃信宗教，希望待人以礼。一次，他碰巧在暑假的第一天下午去拜访他的几位朋友。接下来的六个星期时间就全都是他自己的了——根本就是无事可做。

他闲聊了一会儿，喝了两杯茶，然后硬着头皮，鼓起勇气，突然说道："好吧，我想我……"不过，那家的女主人说："哦，不！琼斯先生，您真的不能再多待一会儿吗？"琼斯总是实话实说。"哦，可以，"他说，"当然，我……呃……可以再待会儿。""那么，请你不要走。”就这样，他留了下来。他喝了 11 杯茶。夜幕降临，他再次站起身来。“好了，”他羞怯地说道：“我想我真的……”

“你非走不可吗？”女主人礼貌地说。“我以为你可能会留下来吃晚饭……”“哦，好吧，我可以留下来吃晚饭的，你知道的，”琼斯说，“虽然……”“那么就请留下来吧，我相信我丈夫会很高兴的。”“好吧，”他声音虚弱地说，“我会留下来的。”然后，他又坐回到椅子上，不停地喝茶，心中苦不堪言。男主人回家了。他们共进晚餐。进餐时，琼斯一直在计划要在八点半离开。这一家人也都很纳闷儿，琼斯先生究竟是在犯傻、生闷气，还是只是在犯傻。

饭后，女主人试图把他从这种状态中“拉”出来，于是她给他看了很多照片。她向他展示了她家“家庭博物馆”的全部展品，其中包括：男主人的叔叔和婶婶的照片、女主人的兄弟和他儿子的照片、女主人的叔叔的朋友身着孟加拉军服拍摄的一张妙趣横生的照片、一张拍摄得美轮美奂的男主人祖父的伴侣狗的照片，以及男主人参加化装舞会时拍摄的一张调皮捣蛋的魔鬼装扮的照片。到了八点半的时候，琼斯已经认真地欣赏了 71 张照片，还有至少大约 69 张照片没来得及看。琼斯再次站起身来。

“我现在必须说晚安了。”他央求着说。“说晚安！”他们说道，“为什么？现在刚刚八点半！您是有其他事情吗？”“没有。”他坦承，并咕哝着要在这里停留六个星期，然后苦笑起来。就在这时，他们发现家里最受宠的孩子，就是那个调皮可爱的小女孩，偏偏把琼斯先生的帽子藏了起来。于是，男主人说琼斯先生必须留下来，并邀请他抽烟斗，再聊会儿天。男主人手里拿着烟斗，跟琼斯聊天。于是，他再次留了下来。其间，他每时每刻都想着壮着胆子道别，但他没有做到。

接下来，男主人开始对琼斯感到厌烦，坐立不安起来，最终用带有讽刺意味的口吻打趣道，琼斯最好留下过夜，这样，他们就可以给他提供一个适应新环境的机会。结果琼斯误解了他的意思，他表示了感谢，眼里闪着泪花。就这样，男主人表面上热情地把琼斯领到了空的房间睡觉，心里却在骂他。

第二天早餐后，男主人出门到城里上班去了，留下琼斯陪婴儿玩。此时琼斯的心都碎了，一点儿勇气都不剩了。一整天，他都在想着离开，但是这个想法也只是在脑袋里闪过，他就是做不到。当男主人晚上回到家时，发现琼斯竟然还在那里，不由得又吃惊又懊恼。他想开个玩笑把他骗出去，于是说，他认为他得向他收取住宿费，嘿嘿！那个不开心的年轻人瞪大眼睛盯着他看了好一会儿，然后紧紧握住了男主人的手，预付了一个月的住宿费，随后就再也控制不住自己的情绪，抽噎呜咽得像个孩子。

在接下来的日子里，他喜怒无常，难以接近。当然，他整日都宅在客厅里，缺少新鲜空气，缺乏锻炼，健康状况每况愈下。一天到晚，他除了喝茶就是看照片。他会连续站着几个小时，凝视着男主人叔叔的朋友穿着孟加拉军服的照片——甚至会对着它说话，有时还会对着它恶毒地咒骂。他的智力显然在衰退。

他终于崩溃了。他们把烧得神志昏迷的他抬到了楼上。接下来，他的病情变得更加严重。他已经不认人了，甚至连穿着孟加拉军服的男主人叔叔的朋友也认不出来了。偶尔，他会突然从惊坐起，尖叫道："好吧，我想我……"然后又倒到枕头上，哈哈大笑，笑声瘆人。然后，他会再一次突然起身，大声喊道："再喝杯茶，再看几张照片！再看几张照片！哈！哈！"

经过一个月的巨大痛苦之后，在他假期的最后一天，他离开了人世。他们说，当最后一刻来临时，他在床上坐起，脸上露出美丽又自信的笑容，然后说道："好吧，天使们在呼唤我。不好意思，我现在真的必须离开了。下午好。"然后，他的灵魂从这幢监狱似的房子里冲了出来，迅疾得如同一只被追赶的猫，从花园围栏一跃而过。

The Awful Fate of Melpomenus Jones

By Stephen Leacock

Some people—not you nor I, because we are so awfully self-possessed—but some people, find great difficulty in saying good-bye when making a call or spending the evening. As the moment draws near when the visitor feels that he is fairly entitled to go away he rises and says abruptly, "Well, I think I..." Then the people say, "Oh, must you go now? Surely it's early yet!" and a pitiful struggle ensues.

I think the saddest case of this kind of thing that I ever knew was that of my poor friend Melpomenus Jones, a curate—such a dear young man, and only twenty-three! He simply couldn't get away from people. He was too modest to tell a lie, and too religious to wish to appear rude. Now it happened that he went to call on some friends of his on the very first afternoon of his summer vacation. The next six weeks were entirely his own—absolutely nothing to do.

He chatted awhile, drank two cups of tea, then braced himself for the effort and said suddenly: “Well, I think I...” But the lady of the house said, “Oh, no! Mr. Jones, can’t you really stay a little longer?” Jones was always truthful. “Oh, yes,” he said, “of course, I—er—can stay.” “Then please don’t go.” He stayed. He drank eleven cups of tea. Night was falling. He rose again. “Well now,” he said shyly, “I think I really...”

“You must go?” Said the lady politely. “I thought perhaps you could have stayed to dinner...” “Oh well, so I could, you know,” Jones said, “if...” “Then please stay, I’m sure my husband will be delighted.” “All right,” he said feebly, “I’ll stay,” and he sank back into his chair, just full of tea, and miserable. Papa came home. They had dinner. All through the meal Jones sat planning to leave at eight-thirty. All the family wondered whether Mr. Jones was stupid and sulky, or only stupid.

After dinner mamma undertook to “draw him out”, and showed him photographs. She showed him all the family museum, several gross of them—photos of papa’s uncle and his wife, and mamma’s brother and his little boy, an awfully interesting photo of papa’s uncle’s friend in his Bengal uniform, an awfully well-taken photo of papa’s grandfather’s partner’s dog, and an awfully wicked one of papa as the devil for a fancy-dress ball. At eight-thirty Jones had examined seventy-one photographs. There were about sixty-nine more that he hadn’t. Jones rose.

“I must say good night now,” he pleaded. “Say good

night!" They said, "why it's only half-past eight! Have you anything to do?" "Nothing," he admitted, and muttered something about staying six weeks, and then laughed miserably. Just then it turned out that the favourite child of the family, such a dear little romp, had hidden Mr. Jones's hat, so papa said that he must stay, and invited him to a pipe and a chat. Papa had the pipe and gave Jones the chat, and still he stayed. Every moment he meant to take the plunge, but couldn't.

Then papa began to get very tired of Jones, and fidgeted and finally said, with jocular irony, that Jones had better stay all night, they could give him a shake-down. Jones mistook his meaning and thanked him with tears in his eyes, and papa put Jones to bed in the spare room and cursed him heartily.

After breakfast next day, papa went off to his work in the City, and left Jones playing with the baby, broken-hearted. His nerve was utterly gone. He was meaning to leave all day, but the thing had got on his mind and he simply couldn't. When papa came home in the evening he was surprised and chagrined to find Jones still there. He thought to jockey him out with a jest, and said he thought he'd have to charge him for his board, he! he! The unhappy young man stared wildly for a moment, then wrung papa's hand, paid him a month's board in advance, and broke down and sobbed like a child.

In the days that followed he was moody and unapproachable.

He lived, of course, entirely in the drawing-room, and the lack of air and exercise began to tell sadly on his health. He passed his time in drinking tea and looking at the photographs. He would stand for hours gazing at the photographs of papa's uncle's friend in his Bengal uniform—talking to it, sometimes swearing bitterly at it. His mind was visibly failing.

At length the crash came. They carried him upstairs in a raging delirium of fever. The illness that followed was terrible. He recognized no one, not even papa's uncle's friend in his Bengal uniform. At times he would start up from his bed and shriek, "Well, I think I..." and then fall back upon the pillow with a horrible laugh. Then, again, he would leap up and cry, "Another cup of tea and more photographs! More photographs! Har! Har!"

At length, after a month of agony, on the last day of his vacation, he passed away. They say that when the last moment came, he sat up in bed with a beautiful smile of confidence playing upon his face, and said, "Well—the angels are calling me. I'm afraid I really must go now. Good afternoon." And the rushing of his spirit from its prison-house was as rapid as a hunted cat passing over a garden fence.

我有病

［英国］哲罗姆·K. 哲罗姆

我还记得那天，到大英博物馆去查阅有关接触性花粉症治疗方面的资料，我猜我大概得了这种小病。我取下一本医书，一口气读完了所有要读的内容。然后，我慵懒地、漫不经心地随便翻着书，泛泛地研究起其他疾病来。我忘记了全神贯注地研究的第一种瘟病是什么病——我知道，是一种可怕的、毁灭性的灾难——没等把一连串的病症征兆看到一半的时候，我便意识到自己肯定得了这种病。

我惊恐万状，万分绝望，没精打采地呆坐了好一会儿。然后又拿起那本书，翻了起来。翻到伤寒——看了看它的各种症状——我发现我又得了伤寒——一定已经染病在身好几个月了，竟然还蒙在鼓里——不知道我还患上其他什么疾病没有；翻到舞蹈病——我发现，正如我预料到的那样，我也患有这种疾病——就这样，我开始对自己的病情产生了兴趣，并决定一查到底，于是我开始按字母顺序逐个排查——翻到疟疾，了解到自己已经出现了疟疾的某些症状，大约在两个星期后就会进入急性发作期；翻到肾小球肾炎，我心中稍微感到一丝安慰，因为我发现我得的只是其中较轻的一种，就目前状况而言，我的生命还可以延续一些年。此外，我还染上了霍乱，并伴有严重的并发症；而我好像是先天性白喉患者。我认认真真地按照 26 个字母挨个儿检查了一遍，得出的结论是，我唯一没有得上的疾病就是髌前囊炎。

起初，我还挺受打击的，心里好像还有那么几分失落。为什么我没有得上髌前囊炎呢？这一缺憾岂不让人不快？不过，过了一会儿，我那贪婪的感觉渐渐平复下来。我回过味儿来了，从药理学讲，我已经把药理学上所罗列的其他各种常见疾病都得了，于是我变得没那么自私了，确认没有得上髌前囊炎也可以接受。反正痛风已经处于恶性晚期了，它好像是在我毫无知觉的情况下找上了我，而我显然是在孩提时期就染上了发酵病。鉴于发酵病是字母表中能查到的最后一种疾病名称，我得出一个结论，我没什么别的病了。

我坐在那里陷入了沉思。我想，从医学角度来看，我一定是一个非常有趣的病例；对于医学院的教学课堂来说，我更是一个极为难得的病例！医学院的学生们有了我的话，他们就没必要再“去医院”实习了。倘若他们有了我的话，我一个人就是他们的“实习医院”。他们只需围着我走一走，然后就可以领他们的毕业证了。

我不知道自己究竟还能活多久，我想自查一下。我摸了摸自己的脉搏。一开始，我一点儿脉象都没摸到。接下来，脉搏突然跳了起来。我掏出怀表，测算脉搏的次数，大概每分钟 147 次。我又摸了摸心脏，却感受不到心脏的跳动。心脏已经停止跳动了。我劝自己相信心脏还在那里，想必还在跳动，只是我这种现象无法解释罢了。我把自己上半身从腰部到头部拍了个遍，还稍微拍了拍身体的侧面和后背，可我却什么也没有摸到，什么也没听到。我想看看自己的舌头，我尽量把舌头伸得长长的，闭上一只眼睛，用另一只眼来检查。我只能看见自己的舌尖，而这么做唯一的收获就是：我比以前更加确信我得了猩红热。

于是，我去看病，我的私人医生是一位老朋友。平时，每当我觉得我生病的时候，他就会摸摸我的脉搏，看看我的舌头，再不咸不淡地谈谈天气；所以我觉得我现在去找他看病是对他的报答。我心中暗想：

"医生需要的就是临床实践，他有了我这样的病人，比拥有一千七百个常见的普通病人得到的临床实践机会还要多，因为这些病人每个人也只能身患一到两种疾病。"于是我径直去找他。他问我：

"你哪里不舒服？"我答道：

"亲爱的伙计，我不会告诉你我得了什么病，浪费你的时间。生命短暂，在我还没说完以前，你就可能离世了。不过，我可以告诉你我没有得什么病，我没有得髌前囊炎。至于我为什么没有得髌前囊炎呢？我说不清楚；然而事实就摆在这里，我没有得髌前囊炎。可是，除此之外，什么病我都有。"

我还把自己是如何发现这些疾病的过程一五一十地讲给他听了。

接下来，他解开我的衣服，俯视着我。他紧握着我的一只手腕，我没料到他会敲打我的胸部——我称之为胆小鬼的做法——又马上把侧着的脸贴到我的身上。最后，他坐下来，开了一个处方，然后把处方折起来递给我。我接了过来揣进衣兜里，走了出去。

我没有打开处方看，就径直来到一家最近的药店把处方递了过去。药剂师看了看处方，又将它退了回来。他说他不收这种处方。

"你是药剂师吧？"我问道。

"我是药剂师啊。如果我经营一个合作商店兼家庭旅馆的话，我倒是可以为你效劳。可我只是一个药剂师，我爱莫能助。"

我看了看那处方，只见上面写道：

"一磅牛排，每隔六小时服用一次；

每天早晨散步十英里；

每天晚上 11 点整准时上床睡觉。

此外不要满脑子装些你不明白的东西。"

The Imaginary Invalid

By Jerome K. Jerome

I remember going to the British Museum one day to read up the treatment for some slight ailment of which I had a touch—hay fever, I fancy it was. I got down the book, and read all I came to read; and then, in an unthinking moment, I idly turned the leaves, and began to indolently study diseases generally. I forget which was the first distemper I plunged into—some fearful, devastating scourge I know—and, before I had glanced half down the list of "premonitory symptoms", it was borne in upon me that I had fairly got it.

I sat for a while, frozen with horror; and then, in the listlessness of despair, I again turned over the pages. I came to typhoid fever—read the symptoms—discovered that I had typhoid fever, must have had it for months without knowing it—wondered what else I had got; turned up St. Vitus's Dance—found, as I expected, that I had that, too, —began to get interested in my case, and determined to sift it to the bottom and so started alphabetically—read up ague, and learned that I was sickening for it, and that the acute stage would commence in about another fortnight. Bright's disease, I was relieved to find, I had only in a modified form, and, so far as that was concerned, I might live for years. Cholera I had, with severe complications; and diphtheria I seemed to have been born with. I plodded conscientiously through the twenty-six letters, and the only malady I could conclude I had not got was housemaid's knee.

I felt rather hurt about this at first; it seemed somehow to be a sort of slight. Why hadn't I got housemaid's knee? Why this invidious reservation? After a while, however, less grasping feelings prevailed. I reflected that I had every other known malady in the pharmacology, and grew less selfish, and determined to do without housemaid's knee. Gout, in its most malignant stage, it would appear, had seized me without my being aware of it; and zymosis I had evidently been suffering with from boyhood. There were no more diseases after zymosis, so I concluded there was nothing else the matter with me.

I sat and pondered. I thought what an interesting case I must be from a medical point of view, what an acquisition I should be to a class! Students would have no need to "walk the hospitals", if they had me, I was a hospital in myself. All they need do would be to walk round me, and, after that, take their diploma.

Then I wondered how long I had to live. I tried to examine myself. I felt my pulse. I could not at first feel any pulse at all.

Then, all of a sudden, it seemed to start off. I pulled out my watch and timed it. I made a hundred and forty-seven to the minute. I tried to feel my heart. I could not feel my heart. It had stopped beating. I have since been induced to come to the opinion that it must have been there all the time, and must have been beating, but I cannot account for it. I patted myself all over my front, from what I call my waist up to my head, and I went a bit round each side, and a little way up the back. But I could not feel or hear anything. I tried to look at my tongue. I stuck it out as far as ever it would go, and I shut one eye, and tried to examine it with the other. I could only see the tip, and the only thing that I could gain from that was to feel more certain than before that I had scarlet fever.

I went to my medical man. He is an old chum of mine, and feels my pulse, and looks at my tongue, and talks about the weather, all for nothing, when I fancy I'm ill, so I thought I would do him a good turn by going to him now. "What a doctor wants," I said, "is practice. He shall have me. He will get more practice out of me than out of seventeen hundred of your ordinary, commonplace patients, with only one or two diseases each." So I went straight up and saw him, and he said:

"Well, what's the matter with you?" I said:

"I will not take up your time, dear boy, with telling you what is the matter with me. Life is brief, and you might pass away before I had finished. But I will tell you what is NOT the matter with me.

I have not got housemaid's knee. Why I have not got housemaid's knee, I cannot tell you, but the fact remains that I have not got it. Everything else, however, I HAVE got."

And I told him how I came to discover it all.

Then he opened me and looked down me, and clutched hold of my wrist, and then he hit me over the chest when I wasn't expecting it—a cowardly thing to do, I call it—and immediately afterward butted me with the side of his head. After that, he sat down and wrote out a prescription, and folded it up and gave it me, and I put it in my pocket and went out.

I did not open it. I took it to the nearest chemist's and handed it in. The man read it and then handed it back. He said he didn't keep it.

I said: "You are a chemist?"

"I am a chemist. If I were a co-operative store and family hotel combined I might be able to oblige you. Being only a chemist hampers me."

I read the prescription. It ran:

"1 lb beefsteak, every 6 hours.

1 ten-mile walk every morning.

1 bed at 11 sharp every night.

And don't stuff up your head with things you don't understand."

情　人

［英国］詹姆斯·伍德

她很喜欢这个湖。温柔而幽深的湖水让她心平气和，带她远离只有小心翼翼才能生存的喧嚣嘈杂的尘世，可以让她无忧无虑地静卧在湖边，心无旁骛地倾听湖水轻轻拍打岸边的声音。

她感受到了安宁。独自一人。无拘无束，自由自在，可以无所事事，只是注视，倾听，梦想。

伦敦，巴黎，纽约——这些地名，也只是地名。这些地名曾经意味着兴奋，接下来是厌倦，然后是挫折，最后是奴役。这些地名曾经把她带到崩溃的边缘，让她怀疑自己的理性。

而这里的一切都很安宁。湖水，树木，小屋。她与它们融为一体。她可以在这里度过余生，她在这里可以幸福地死去。

一团乌云匆匆地掠过太阳，如同一支更为庞大、更为精锐的部队的先头部队。一股清新的风儿吹过，湖面上骤起层层涟漪，从湖的那一边急速散开来，几乎要浸湿她的脚。一只秃鼻乌鸦，发出寂寞、焦虑不安的叫声，从她头顶孤独地飞过。东边也响起了隆隆的雷鸣。

她赶紧收拾东西，直奔小屋。身后，雨下了起来，湖面涟漪斑驳。雨点拍打着树叶，她在树下飞跑。跑到屋前门的时候，雨水已经打湿了衣衫，人也气喘吁吁了。当她推开门的时候，暴风雨来了。

壁炉旁赫然立着一人，面容憔悴，神情冷淡。

“嗨！”

对一个擅自闯入的陌生人如此打招呼，显然有些奇怪。但这是她唯一能想到的。她对那些盼望和等待她的人，这是她的惯常做法。莫非这就是这里人的行为方式？

“我想，你是来避雨的吧？”她问道。

但那个男人却一声没吭。

这是侵犯隐私私闯民宅的行为，她本应感到生气，但恼怒似乎没有任何意义。现在，这间屋子、壁炉仿佛都是那个男人的，她自己反倒像一个来到别人家避雨的人了。

她注视着他，开始小心翼翼起来，同时等他做个解释。但那个男人还是一声不吭，一个字也没有。

“你淋湿了吧？”

他站在那里，蜷缩在火堆旁，眼睛直勾勾地盯着快要熄灭的死灰。

她走了过去，与他擦肩而过，她弯腰把木柴拨了拨，让火烧得旺些。火焰时不时地迸发出来，照亮了他深色眸子里的悲伤。

“跪下来，点燃这座将要熄灭的壁炉

燃烧的火焰让整个小屋变得温暖……”

他用安静的、平板单调的语气说出这些话，让她大吃一惊。

“你说什么？”她问道。

可是，他似乎没有听见她说的话。只有风在树上的颤动和雨打在屋顶上的滴答声打破了这怪异的寂静。

她又试了试，“天快黑了，你还想再坐一会儿吗？”

她过去脱下了大衣，梳了梳头发，他的目光追随着她的一举一动。

“……从她的身上

脱下了湿漉漉的斗篷和披肩，

把沾满泥土的手套放在一旁，摘下了

她的帽子，让湿漉漉的头发倾泻而下……”

诗歌。他在吟诵诗歌。

他看起来有点儿像诗人，瘦削，痛苦，眼神里有一种苦涩，形体上有绝望。他的声音低沉而慵懒，如同湖中央湖水最幽暗的地方。

不过，这些诗行不是他写就的，这些词不是他创造的，听起来有些熟悉，依稀记得，肯定是以前听过吧？

“这是你写的？”她问道，强迫自己打开话匣子。

他微微一笑，一个我见犹怜的微笑，却没有说话。

她注视着他，心中有一种感觉，他擅自走进这个小屋，他知道她会回到这个小屋里。他在等她。他在期待她。她对此深信不疑。不仅如此，她第一次感到了害怕。

她转头看着窗外。窗外没有人，只有雨水不停地敲打的声音。

她知道她到不了村庄，她知道，就算她大声呼救，也不会有人听得见。她就是孤身一人，完完全全的孤身一人与这个吓人的、一声不吭的陌生人在一起。

突然，外面什么东西破裂的声音把她吓得跳了起来：一棵树被劈开，接着倒在了地上。

“为了泄愤撕裂了这棵榆树的树梢

为了扰乱这一池湖水，穷凶极恶……”

又是那首诗！就是那首诗！叫什么来着？为什么与此情此景契合得这么天衣无缝？她怎么就想不起来了呢？

“多么可怕的风啊。”她尽量显得漫不经心地说道。“或许我应该保证……”

她往门口走去，他转过头来，慢慢地摇了摇头。

她停下了脚步。仿佛被催眠了一般。无法远离他一步。

宿命，她的大脑告诉她。这就是你的宿命。这就是造你的目的。伦敦，巴黎，纽约——不论你去过什么地方，你终归都会回到这里，回到这个小屋，回到这个男人身边。

静静地，他向她走来，从她身旁经过，走向那扇沉重的橡木门。锁头里的钥匙拧了拧，窗户上的百叶静静地拉上了。

温柔地，非常温柔地，他拉着她的一只胳膊，把她领到了壁炉和熊熊燃烧的炉火旁。只有他们两个，她想尖叫，却叫不出来。

“最后，她坐在我身旁

呼唤着我……”

那首诗！那首该死的诗！接下来怎么样了呢？求求你，上帝，接下来怎么样了呢？求求你，求求你，让她想起来吧！

“……没有回音

她把我的胳膊放到了她的腰上

露出了她光滑白嫩的肩胛……”

他的左手紧紧地抓着她，修长的手指掐进了她的皮肤，与此同时，他摩挲着她柔软的金发。

“然而激情时而会占上风

也无法遏制今夜欢乐的盛宴

一个突如其来的念头是如此苍白

因为爱她……”

爱情？这不是爱情！这是疯狂。是精神病。他疯了。他把某种美丽的事物扭曲成了恐怖的死亡现实。

“我确实抬头凝视着她的眼睛……”

他自己的眼睛里闪烁出一丝狂热的光芒。

“我终于快乐而自豪地知悉

血紫质症爱慕我……”

血紫质症！勃朗宁的诗！她想起来啦！哦，我的上帝，不！不要！不要！

“那一刻，她是我的，我的金发碧眼的俏佳人

至纯至善……”

她想尖叫。她尝试着尖叫。她却做不到。他的手指扼住了她的喉咙，叫不出声。她挣扎着呼吸，却感觉自己的身体在坠落，坠落。她的意识挣扎着要逃离黑暗，却只能听到一个人的声音，一个遥远的声音，越来越远，令人迷醉……

“……她所有的头发

被我拧成了一根长长的金带

在她娇小的喉咙上绕了三圈

勒死了她……”

The Lover

By James Wood

She was glad of the lake. It's soft, dark water helped to soothe and quiet her mind. It took her away from the noisy, squawkish world of the cat-walk and let her lie untroubled at its side, listening only to the gentle lapping of its waves.

She felt at peace. Alone. Unhindered and free. Free to do nothing but watch and listen and dream.

London, Paris, New York—names, only names. Names that had once meant excitement, then boredom, then frustration, then slavery. Names that had brought her to the edge of a breakdown and left her doubting her own sanity.

But here everything was at peace. The lake, the trees, the cottage. And she was at one with them. Here she could stay for the rest of her life. Here she would be happy to die.

Across the sun hurried a darkening filter of cloud; the advance guard of a larger and even graver army. The ripples on the water, chased by a freshening wind, pushed their way anxiously from the far side of the lake until they almost bounced at her feet. Way above her a solitary rook cawed its way home—a lonely, troubled sound. And in the East there was thunder.

Quickly she gathered her things together and made for the cottage. But already the rain flecked the water behind her and pattered the leaves as she raced beneath the trees. Sodden and breathless, she ran for the cottage door, and, as she opened it, the storm burst.

And there on the hearth, gaunt and unwelcome, stood a man.

"Hello!"

It was an odd way to greet a complete stranger who had invaded her home, but it was all she could think of to say. A casual greeting to someone who seemed to be expecting her, waiting for her. Maybe it was the way they did things down here?

"I suppose you had to shelter from the storm, too?" she asked.

The man said nothing.

She ought to have been angry at this rude intrusion on her privacy, but anger somehow seemed pointless. It was as if the cottage was his, the hearth was his, and she had come out of the storm to seek refuge at his door.

She watched him, cautiously, waiting for an explanation. He said nothing. Not a word.

"Did you get wet?" she asked.

He stood, huddled by the open fire, gazing at the dying embers.

She walked over, brushing against him as she bent to stir the logs into life, but still he did not move. Erratically the flames burst forth, lighting up the sadness in his dark eyes.

"And kneeled and made the cheerless grate
Blaze up and all the cottage warm..."

The words, spoken by him in a quiet, toneless voice, took her by surprise.

"Pardon?" she said.

But he seemed not to hear. Only the shiver of wind in the trees and the tittering of rain on the thatched roof broke that eerie silence.

She tried once more. "It looks as if it's set in for the evening. Would you like to sit down for a while?"

His eyes followed her as she moved to take off her coat and brush out her hair.

"...and from her form
Withdrew the dripping cloak and shawl,
And laid her soiled gloves by, untied
Her hat and let the damp hair fall..."

Poetry. He was quoting poetry.

He looked vaguely like a poet; lean, distressed, with a certain bitterness in his eyes and hopelessness in his form. And his voice was deep and languid, like the middle of the lake where the water ran darkest.

Yet those were not his lines. The words were not created by him. They were somehow familiar. Half remembered. Surely she had heard them before?

"Did you write that?" she asked, forcing herself to make conversation.

He smiled, a pitiful smile, but did not answer.

As she watched him she had the feeling that he'd let himself into the cottage knowing that she would return. He'd been waiting for her. Expecting her. She was sure of it. And, for the first time, she was afraid.

She turned towards the window. No one was outside. Just the rain beating unceasingly.

She knew she'd never make it to the village, and no one would hear if she cried out. She was alone, completely alone with this frighteningly silent stranger.

A sudden renting sound outside made her jump: a splintering of wood followed by a crashing to the ground.

"It tore the elm tops down for spite

And did its worst to vex the lake..."

That poem again! That same poem! What was it? Why did it fit the scene so perfectly? And why couldn't she remember it?

"What an awful wind," she said as casually as possibly. "Perhaps I ought to make sure that..."

She had been working her way towards the door when he

turned and slowly shook his head.

She stopped. Hypnotised. Unable to take another step away from him.

Destiny, her mind told her. This is your destiny; what you were created for. London, Paris, New York—no matter where you went you had to return here. To this cottage. To this man.

Quietly he walked towards her, past her, and on towards the heavy oak door. The key twisted in the lock, the shutters closed silently over the windows.

Gently, very gently, he took her arm and led her back to the hearth and the blazing fire. They were alone and she wanted to scream, but she couldn't.

"And last she sat down by my side
And called me..."

That poem! That damned poem! How did it go? Please God, how did it go? Please, please let her remember!

"...when no voice replied
She put my arm about her waist
And made her smooth white shoulder bare..."

His left arm held her tightly, the slender fingers biting into her skin, while his right hand caressed the softness of her fair hair.

"But passion sometimes would prevail
Nor could tonight's gay feast restrain
A sudden thought of one so pale

For love of her..."

Love? This wasn't love! This was madness. Insanity. He was crazy. He'd taken something of beauty and twisted it into macabre reality.

"Be sure I looked up at her eyes..."

His own eyes shone with a maniacal fervour.

"Happy and proud at last I knew
Porphyria worshipped me..."

Porphyria! Browning's poem! She knew it! Oh my god, no! No! No!

"That moment she was mine, mine fair
Perfectly pure and good..."

She wanted to scream. She tried to scream. But she couldn't. His fingers were about her throat and no sound emerged. She fought for air but she could feel her body falling, falling. Her mind struggled to escape from the darkness but all she could hear was a voice, a distant voice, fading, ecstatic...

"...and all her hair
In one long yellow string I wound
Three times her little throat around
And strangled her..."

南方男人

［英国］罗尔德·达尔

快到晚上六点了，我想到了为自己买杯啤酒，然后出去躺在游泳池边的躺椅上，享受落日余晖的时间。就在这时，我注意到一位身材矮小的老人正沿游泳池边轻快地走着。他穿着一身整洁的白色西装，走路速度很快，步子很大，脚尖儿一踮一踮的。

他停在我身边，微笑着，露出两排极小的参差不齐、颜色暗淡的牙齿。我也对他回敬以微笑。“打扰了，我可以坐在这儿吗？”“当然可以，”我说，“请坐。”“傍晚的天气多好啊。”他说。“在牙买加这地方，每天傍晚的天气都很好。”我无法肯定他的口音像意大利语还是西班牙语，但我相当肯定他是来自南美。而且，当你靠近些看他时，你就会发现他的确很老了，大概68岁或70岁的样子。“说的没错，”我说，“这里的天气很棒，不是吗？”

突然，一个美国男孩站到了我们面前。他刚从游泳池出来，浑身湿漉漉的，旁边还站着一位英国女孩。“这些椅子有人坐吗？”他说。“没人。”我回答。“介意我坐下吗？”“坐吧。”“谢谢。”他说。他给女孩递烟，女孩拒绝了，然后他又给我递香烟，我拿了一支。那个小老头说：“谢谢你，可是不了，我想我带了雪茄。”他掏出一盒鳄鱼牌雪茄盒，取出一支，然后又拿出一把带着一个小剪刀的小刀，接着用剪刀剪断了雪茄尾端。

“来，让我来给您个火吧。”那个美国男孩举起他的打火机。“有风，这玩意儿点不着！”“没事儿，能点着。而且一直都能。”“一直都能？”小老头轻声问道。“当然啦，而且万无一失。反正，我点的时候是这样。” “我们打个小小的赌如何，就赌你的打火机能不能打着火，怎么样？”“没问题，这赌我打了，”男孩说道，“为什么不呢！”“跟我打赌，赌注要大。我很有钱，而且很喜欢赌博。听我说，我的车就停在酒店外面。车子非常好。是一辆你们美国产的汽车，凯迪拉克。你只要连续成功打着十次打火机，那辆凯迪拉克就是你的了。你想要那辆凯迪拉克，是吧？”

“当然，我想要一辆凯迪拉克。”那男孩露齿而笑，说道。“好的。那好。那我们就打赌，我的赌注是那辆凯迪拉克。”“那我该赌什么？”男孩问。“也许是你左手的小手指。”“我的什么？！”男孩的笑容不再有了。“是的。为什么不呢？你赢了，你开走我的车。你输了，我带走那根手指。”“我不明白。你是什么意思？你要带走我的手指吗？”“我把它砍掉。”“天哪！这个赌注太疯狂了！”“好吧，好吧，好吧，”小老头说，“我搞不懂，你既然说打火机能打着，但你又不肯打赌。那就忘了这个赌局，好吧？”

一片寂静。我可以看出小老头已经用他的荒谬提议成功地让男孩不安起来。很明显，男孩的内心开始有些紧张起来。“现在，让我跟你核对一下这个赌注吧。”男孩最后说道。“你说如果我连续十次成功地打着这个打火机，我会赢得一辆凯迪拉克；如果这十次里有任何一次失败了，代价就是我左手的小指。对吗？”

“当然。就是这个赌。不过我觉得你害怕了。”男孩只停顿了片刻，他先扫了一眼那个英国女孩，然后又扫了我一眼。“好吧，”他直截了当地说道，“我跟你赌。”“好！”小老头平静地拍了一下手。“很好，”他说，“我们这就开始。先生，你，”他转向我说，“有劳你当个裁判。”我可以看到他苍白的脸、亮晶晶的黑色的瞳孔和呆滞的眼睛。“好吧，”我说，“我会奉陪，但我声明我并不喜欢这场赌局。”“你也来吧，”小老头对女孩说，“过来看看。”

我们都进了小老头的房间，坐在一张桌子旁，然后小老头开始将男孩的左手绑在桌子上。绑完以后，他也坐在了桌子旁，手里拿着一把斧头。“我们都准备好了吗？”他说。“裁判先生，你要说开始。”

“你准备好了吗？”我问那个男孩。“我准备好了。”他回答说。“你呢？”我问小老头。“准备得好好的了。”他回答说，同时把斧头举到距离男孩手指上方约两英尺的位置，做好了砍下去的准备。男孩眼睛盯着斧头，但他并没有表现出退缩，嘴也没有动。他只是扬起了眉毛，皱起了眉头。“好吧，”我说，“开始！”

“一！”我喊道。火焰没有熄灭。“二！”打火机再次点燃。除了我，谁都一声不吭。男孩的眼睛一直盯着打火机。小老头在空中高举着斧头，同时也看着打火机，“三！”“四！”“五！”“六！”“七！”“八！”我说着。而就在此时，门开了。

我们都转过身来。我们看到一个身材矮小、黑色头发的很老的老太太站在门口。她在那里站了大约两秒钟后，突然冲进屋来喊道：“卡洛斯！卡洛斯！卡洛斯！”她一把抓住小老头的手腕，夺下斧头扔在床上，抓起小老头白色西装的翻领，开始使劲儿地摇晃他，与此同时，一直用类似西班牙语跟他讲话，语速快，声音大，言辞激烈。接下来，她把他拖到房间的另一头，并把他推倒在一张床上。

“我很抱歉，”那个女人说，“发生这样的事情，我真的非常抱歉。”

她的英语说得几乎完美。“太糟糕了，”她接着说，“我觉得这的确是我的错。我就是去洗了个头，让他一个人待了十分钟。我回来却发现，他又故伎重施了。”她看起来非常难过，深感忧虑。

男孩正从桌子上解自己的手，我和那个英国女孩则站在那里无言以对。“他是个危险的人。”女人说。“我们还住老家时，他就总共砍掉了四十七个人的四十七根手指，还输了十一辆汽车。最后，他们威胁要把他关在什么地方。这就是我把他带到这里的原因。我猜他跟你赌了一辆车吧。”女人说。“是的，”男孩回答道，“一辆凯迪拉克。”“他没有车。那是我的车。”她说。“他跟你打赌时甚至连赌注都没有，这就更糟糕了。我感到非常惭愧，真是太抱歉了。”此时，她看上去是一位非常善良的女人。

“我们只是打了个小赌。”小老头咕哝道。“他没有什么赌注可下。”女人说。“他在这个世界上一无所有，一无所有。事实上，很久以前，我从他那里赢来了这一切。这需要时间，旷日持久，过程艰辛，但我最终赢得了这一切。”她抬头看着男孩，她微微一笑，是一种迟缓而哀伤的笑容。直到现在，她的那只手还会浮现在我眼前——上面只剩下一根手指和一根大拇指。

Man from the South

By Roald Dahl

It was getting on toward six o'clock so I thought I'd buy myself a beer and go out and sit in a deck chair by the swimming pool and have a little evening sun. Just then I noticed a small, oldish man walking briskly around the edge of the pool. He was immaculately dressed in a white suit and he walked very quickly with little bouncing strides, pushing himself high up onto his toes with each step.

He stopped beside me and smiled, showing two rows of very small, uneven teeth, slightly tarnished. I smiled back. "Excuse pleess, but may I sit here?" "Certainly," I said. "Go ahead." "A fine evening," he said. "They are all evenings fine here in Jamaica." I couldn't tell if the accent were Italian or Spanish, but I felt fairly sure he was some sort of a South American. And old, too, when you saw him close. Probably around sixty-eight or seventy. "Yes," I said. "It is wonderful here, isn't it?"

Suddenly an American boy was standing in front of us. He was dripping wet from the pool and one English girl was standing there with him. "Are these chairs taken?" He said. "No," I answered. "Mind if I sit down?" "Go ahead." "Thanks," he said. He offered his cigarettes to the girl and she refused; then he offered them to me and I took one. The little man said, "Thank you, no, but I tink I have a cigar." He pulled out a crocodile case and got himself a cigar, then he produced a knife which had a small scissor in it and he snipped the end of the cigar.

"Here, let me give you a light." The American boy held up his lighter. "Dat will not work in dis wind." "Sure, it'll work. It always works." "All-ways?" the little man said softly. "Sure, it never fails. Not with me anyway." "Shall we not make a little bet on whether your lighter lights?" "Sure, I'll bet," the boy said. "Why not?" "I make you very good bet. I am rich man and I am sporting man also. Listen to me. Outside de hotel iss my car. Iss very fine car. American car from your country, Cadillac. You strike lighter successfully ten times running and Cadillac is yours. You like to have dis Cadillac, yes?"

"Sure, I'd like to have a Cadillac." The boy was grinning. "All right. Fine. We make a bet and I put up my Cadillac." "And what do I put up?" Said the boy. "Perhaps, de little finger of your left hand." "My what!" the boy stopped grinning. "Yes. Why not? You win, you take de car. You looss, I take de finger." "I don't get it. How do you mean, you take the finger?" "I chop it off." "Jumping jeepers! That's a crazy bet!" "Well, well, well," he said. "I do not understand. You say it lights but you will not bet. Den we forget it, yes?"

There was a silence, and I could see that the little man has succeeded in disturbing the boy with his absurd proposal. It was obvious that a small tension was beginning to build up inside him. "Now just let me check up on this bet of yours," he said at last. "You say if I make this lighter light ten times running I win a Cadillac. If it misses just once then I forfeit the little finger of my left hand. Is that right?"

"Certainly. Dat is de bet. But I tink you are afraid." The boy paused for just a moment and he glanced first at the English girl, then at me. "Yes," he said sharply. "I'll bet you." "Good!" The little man clapped his hands together quietly, once. "Fine," he said. "We do it now. And you, sir," he turned to me, "you would perhaps be good enough to, what you call it, to-to referee." He had pale, almost colourless eyes with tiny bright black pupils. "All right," I said. "I'll come along but I don't like the bet." "You come, too," he said to the girl. "You come and watch."

We all went to the little man's room, sat at a table, and the little man started tying up the boy's left hand to the table. When he'd finished that, he positioned himself beside the table with a chopper in his hand. "We are all ready?" He said. "Mister referee, you must say to begin."

"Are you ready?" I asked the boy. "I'm ready." He said. "And you?" I asked the little man. "Quite ready," he said and he lifted the chopper up in the air and held it there about two feet above the boy's finger, ready to chop. The boy watched it, but he didn't flinch and his mouth didn't move at all. He merely raised his eyebrows and frowned. "All right," I said. "Go ahead."

"One!" I called. The flame did not blow out. "Two!" The lighter lighted again. No one else said anything. The boy kept his eyes on the lighter. The little man held the chopper up in the air and he also was watching the lighter. "Three!" "Four!" "Five!" "Six!" "Seven!" "Eight!" I said, and as I said it the door opened.

We all turned and we saw a woman standing in the doorway, a small, black-haired woman, rather old, who stood there for about two seconds then rushed forward shouting, "Carlos! Carlos!" She grabbed his wrist, took the chopper from him, threw it on the bed, took hold of the little man by the lapels of his white suit and began shaking him very vigorously, talking to him fast and loud and fiercely all the time in some Spanish-sounding language. Then she hauled him across the room and pushed him backward onto one of the beds.

"I am so sorry," the woman said. "I am so terribly sorry that this should happen." She spoke almost perfect English. "It is too bad," she went on. "I suppose it is really my fault. For ten minutes I leave him alone to go and have my hair washed and

I come back and he is at it again." She looked sorry and deeply concerned.

The boy was untying his hand from the table. The English girl and I stood there and said nothing. "He is a menace," the woman said. "Down where we live at home he has taken altogether forty-seven fingers from different people, and he has lost eleven cars. In the end they threatened to have him put away somewhere. That's why I brought him up here. I suppose he bet you a car," the woman said. "Yes," the boy answered. "A Cadillac." "He has no car. It's mine. And that makes it worse," she said, "that he should bet you when he has nothing to bet with. I am ashamed and very sorry about it all." She seemed an awfully nice woman.

"We were only having a little bet," mumbled the little man. "He hasn't anything left to bet with," the woman said. "He hasn't a thing in the world. Not a thing. As a matter of fact, I myself won it all from him a long while ago. It took time, a lot of time, and it was hard work, but I won it all in the end." She looked up at the boy and she smiled, a slow sad smile. I can see it now, that hand of hers; it had only one finger on it, and a thumb.

返璞归真

［西班牙］费尔南多·索伦蒂诺

我是这种人：对于社会学家或精神分析师在电视圆桌会议上提出的任何想法，我都倾向于立刻照单全收。在眼镜、胡须和烟斗烟雾中涌现出来的、深沉而无可争辩的男性声音提出，现代人已经被物质化了，并且一点儿一点儿地为消费社会所消费。

我吓坏了，心理过程就是头晕目眩——虽然没有必要描述，但是很容易想象——这驱使我立即关掉电视，赶紧跑到乌尔基扎别墅附近的苏州赫尔马诺斯自行车店。我不知道那里有多少萨索里奥兄弟，因为店里只有一个瘦骨嶙峋、颧骨高高的人，事实证明他聪明伶俐、办事高效、反应迅速。

当他把自行车卖给我的时候，他说了几句老师会对弟子说的话：“这是你能做的最明智的事情。生活变得毫无希望地复杂起来。自行车是简单的，尽管它是一种机械装置，但它需要自然的东西：新鲜空气、阳光和运动。”

我认同。我感到孩童般的快乐，我骑上自行车，在乌尔基扎别墅和佩雷顿别墅的街道上走着。几分钟后，我在埃尔帕洛马圣多斯卢加雷斯的林奇别墅前停了下来。“太神奇了。”我自言自语道。“这种简单而累人的交通工具能让我在相当短的时间内走这么远的路。”是的，但是我到底走了多远呢？

因为我厌恶不精确和猜测，所以我又去见了萨索里奥先生。这一次他用严肃而迟疑的神情看着我，他的态度似乎有了明显的转变：

“记住，”他说，“回来是你的主意。”

我简洁地奉承道：

“一个满意的顾客总会回到诚实的商人那里。”

我问他是否认为给自行车安个里程表是个好主意。

他责骂我：“没有速度计的里程表就像没有刀的叉子，它们互相补充，一个给另一个存在的理由。里程表会告诉你你走了多远，速度计会让你知道你在空挡有多强。”

我承认他说的是对的，几分钟后，这两个装置就安在我自行车的把手上了。

“人们要么沉浸在自己的世界里，要么就是傻瓜。”萨索里奥先生说道。“所以撞上个心不在焉的人一点儿也不奇怪，要不买个电铃，凑个三件套？”

“对不起，我不同意你的看法，我讨厌汽车的喇叭声。”

“这个电铃来自日不落帝国，”他又开始上课了，“也许你知道日本人试图节省空间。这个电铃比一个火柴盒还小，即使你不欣赏城市号喇叭的旋律，你仍然可以欣赏附带的设备：一个带有播放和录音功能的盒式磁带的手提式录音机，一个显示东京、亚的斯亚贝巴和特古西加尔巴标准时间的钟面式风向指示器，一个温度和气压显示器，一个具有57个功能的迷你计算器，如果你需要的话，足可以走一路算一路。”

鉴于所有这些特色功能，我欢天喜地地买下了电铃。

“天气怎么样？”萨索里奥先生接着问道。

这是一个修辞问题。

“这真是太棒了，一个阳光灿烂的日子。”他自问自答道。“一月份在布宜诺斯艾利斯，任何运气够好的人都会心烦意乱。但是，当你在荒郊野外遇到一场大暴风雨时，当你穿的衣服和鞋子装了一千加仑的水回家时，不要感到奇怪。”

一时间，我懵圈了。

他补充道：“在 21 世纪的门槛上，有了这个小装置，哪个白痴会让自己淋湿呢？”他手心里托着一种小型电视机样的东西。“它能预测未来七十二小时的天气变化，零误差。”

他迅速把它拧到车把上。

“它还可以显示澳大利亚和加蓬的等压线和等降雨线，提供波斯湾潮汐的信息，并配有一个超声波系统，可以消灭在路上等待骑车人的豪猪、野狗和鬣鳞蜥。”

“那蚊子和苍蝇呢？”

“不幸的是，可恶的双翅目昆虫已经对这种装置的万无一失的射线产生了免疫力。但这又算得了什么呢？当它在任何种类的纸上只能复制一两个侧面的颜色。”

“后挡泥板，”萨索里奥先生说，“不应该感觉不如车把手。车把上有这么多奇妙的装备，后面却空无一物。”

他在后座安装了一个黄油碟大小的金属盒子，里面有按钮和杠杆。

“你有点儿懒散，很可能是暴饮暴食的结果，吃货一个。当走在路上出现强烈的饥饿感时，有什么比这个红外线烤箱更适合蒸馏器把空气中的湿气变成勃艮第酒，同时在 25 秒内用土豆和洋葱搭配烤鸡肉或牛肉片的呢？”

这个提议很诱人，我不够坚强，无法抗拒。

“我出生在这个城市，我在乌尔基扎别墅住了 53 年，”他抬高了嗓门儿和右臂，自言自语道，“我一直以为这个社区就像一个大家庭。你看起来不猥琐，所以我愿意承担风险，相信你是个老实人。我会给你美元贷款，36 个月内你可以轻松地分期付款。为了省事，免得你往我实验室跑麻烦，把你的地址给我，其实我已经记住了，明天我的财务经理会带一些文件到你家让你签字。”

我手颤抖着在报纸的空白处写下了地址，担心他会忘记他的承诺，于是追问道：“他明天一定会来的，对吧？”

“他一定会去的。他会背带着本票，哭着喊着要破产签名，还有其他高科技的宣传册，这会让你大跌眼镜的。我再次祝贺你，这是你能做的最明智的事情。生活变得毫无希望地复杂起来，自行车却简单而自然。”

我感激涕零，答道：“非常感谢。”

我骑着自行车离开了：快乐，充满活力，嘴里还哼着小曲儿。

Going Back to Our Roots

By Fernando Sorrentino

I tend to instantly accept any idea proposed by a sociologist or psychoanalyst during televised round tables. Emerging among eyeglasses, beards and pipe smoke, the deep and indisputable male voice propounded that modern humans have been objectified and that little by little, the consumer society has been consuming them.

I got scared and a dizzying mental process—which there is no point in describing, but which is easily imagined—propelled me to immediately turn off the television and hurry to the Suasorio Hermanos bicycle shop in my neighborhood of Villa Urquiza. I do not know how many Suasorio brothers there are as there was only one very thin man with high cheekbones in the shop; he turned out to be clever, efficient and quick.

As he was selling me the bicycle, he let fall a few sentences of the kind a teacher would say to a disciple:

"This is the best thing you could have done. Life has become hopelessly complicated. A bicycle is simple, and even though it is a mechanical device, it entails natural things: fresh air, sunshine and exercise."

I agreed. Feeling rather childishly happy, I got on the bicycle and headed out on the streets of Villa Urquiza and Villa Pueyrredón; after a few minutes I ended up in Villa Lynch, in Santos Lugares, in El Palomar. "Amazing," I said to myself. "This simple and ascetic vehicle lets me cover long distances in a fairly short time." Yes, but how far did I really go?

Since I abhor imprecision and conjecture, I went to see Mr. Suasorio again. This time he looked at me with a serious and uncertain air; there seemed to be a perceptible shift in his attitude:

"Remember," he said, "it was your idea to come back."

I answered with sententious flattery:

"A satisfied customer always returns to an honest merchant."

I asked whether he thought it would be a good idea to improve the bicycle with an odometer.

He scolded me, "An odometer without a speedometer is like a fork without a knife; they complement each other and one gives the other a reason to exist. The odometer will tell you how far you've traveled and the speedometer will let you know how strong your idle le are."

I admitted he was right and in a few minutes, the two devices were attached to the handlebars of my bicycle.

"People wander about engrossed in themselves or they are

born fools," said Mr. Suasorio. "So don't be surprised if you run into some absent minded person. How about an electric horn to round out a terrific trio?"

"I'm sorry to disagree with you, but I hate the honking of horns."

"This horn comes from the Empire of the Rising Sun," he lectured, "and perhaps you know that the Japanese try to save space. This is no larger than a matchbox and even if you don't appreciate the melody of a honking urban horn, you can still enjoy the extras: a boom box with cassette player and recorder, a wind clock showing the official time in Tokyo, Addis Ababa and Tegucigalpa, a temperature and atmospheric pressure indicator and a fifty seven function mini calculator in case you need to do sums along the way."

Given all those features, I was very happy to buy the horn.

"What about the weather?" asked Mr. Suasorio next.

It was a rhetorical question.

"It's wonderful, a radiant day," he answered himself. "January in Buenos Aires fries the brains of anyone lucky enough to have any. But don't be surprised when you get caught in a savage storm in the most desolate spot and return home with a thousand gallons of water in your clothes and shoes."

I puzzled for a moment.

He added, "On the threshold of the 21st century, would

anyone who is not an idiot let himself get wet when there is this little device?" He held a kind of Lilliputian television set in the palm of his hand. "It predicts changes in weather seventy-two hours in advance and with zero margin of error."

He rapidly screwed it onto the handlebars.

"It also shows isobars and isohyets for Australia and Gabon, gives you information on tides in the Persian Gulf and has an ultrasonic system that exterminates the porcupines, wild dogs and iguanas that lie in wait for cyclists on the roads."

"What about mosquitoes and flies?"

"Unfortunately, the despicable dipterans have developed immunity to the foolproof rays of this device. But what does that matter, when it also makes copies that are one—or two sided, in color and on any kind of paper?"

"The rear fender," noted Mr. Suasorio, "shouldn't feel inferior to the handlebars. There are all these wonders on the handlebars and nothing in the back."

He mounted a butter dish sized metal box with buttons and levers behind the seat:

"You're a bit of a slacker and you probably over-eat and enjoy your food. When fierce hunger pangs strike en route, is there anything better than this infrared oven for roasting a chicken or a cut of beef with potatoes and onions in only twenty-five seconds while the distillers turn the moisture in the air into Burgundy wine?"

The offer was tempting and I was not strong enough to resist.

"I was born in this town, I've lived in Villa Urquiza for fifty-three years," he proffered, raising his voice and his right arm, "and I have always thought that the neighborhood is like a big family. You don't look sneaky, so I'll risk it and trust that you're honest. I'll give you credit in dollars, to be paid off in thirty-six easy monthly installments. To save you the trouble of going to my laboratory, give me your address, which I already know by heart, and tomorrow my financial manager will go to your house with some documents for you to sign."

I shakily wrote the address in the margin of a newspaper. Fearing he would forget his promise, I urged: "He will come tomorrow for sure, right?"

"Of course he'll come. He'll be bearing promissory notes crying out for bankrupt signatures and brochures for other scientific advances that will make your jaw drop. I congratulate you once more; this is the best thing you could have done. Life has become hopelessly complicated and a bicycle is simple and natural."

Moved, I answered, "Thank you so much."

I mounted and pedaled away: happy, full of life and with a song on my lips.

免费的午餐

［英国］杰克·奥尔索普

“早上好，先生们。我是卡多扎，随时为您服务！”

他打招呼的这队人是一群女性，但卡多扎并不为此烦恼。他为自己年轻时学过的英语感到骄傲。他的语速很快，全程面带微笑。不幸的是，他很少听懂别人对他说的话，但他也没有为此而烦恼。

女人们直勾勾地盯着他看，不知道他是官员还是疯子。

“欢迎来到卢班戈。欢迎光临大酒店。如有需要，就问卡多扎！”

领队断定他是一位官员。“我们是来参加会议的，同志可……”

“卡多扎。C-A-R-D-O-S-A。 我是安哥拉人。欢迎你们！”

她看了看他。显而易见，他是个欧洲人，也可能是独立后留下来的葡萄牙人。“我们是来参加会议的。”

“啊，是的，一个美丽的国家。”卡多扎笑容满面地说。

这些女人来自朝鲜，对自己的英语水平并不自信。她们不知道是自己听不懂卡多扎说的话，还是他不明白她们的话。

“朝鲜。” 领队犹犹豫豫地说。“我们是来参加贸易联盟大会的。”

卡多扎又笑了笑。他听懂了“大会”（congress），在葡萄牙语里几乎是同一个词。“啊，好的，大会！请跟我来，先生们。”

女人们面面相觑，然后看了看卡多扎。他张开双臂。“不要担心！我认识路。我带你们去会议室。”他在前面带路，女人们看到也没有更好的选择了，于是跟在他后面。他一边走一边回头继续谈话。“很高兴见到你们。你们好！有什么需要吗？出租车，香烟，吃的，喝的……问卡多扎就好啦。”

“我们是朝鲜代表团。”领队说。“你是谁？”

“我很好。”卡多扎回答。

“你是我们的向导吗？”

他看了看表。尽管表已经停了，但戴在他的手腕上却很好看。“八点半！”他胸有成竹地说。领队看了看她的同事，摇了摇头。

他把代表团带到会议室，深深鞠了一躬。“再见。一会儿见，呃，同志们。”

快中午的时候，会议结束了，她们从会议室出来，卡多扎正等着她们。“很好！你们已经讨论过了，现在必须得吃饭。跟我来。”他带她们往餐厅走时，领队再次尝试打探卡多扎的身份。

“你是政府官员吗，卡多扎同志？”

“不错。是的，这儿的食物很好吃。你们会喜欢的！”

在专门为她们准备的长餐桌前，他坐在了领队旁边。

“这个，”他用叉子尖儿举着一种灰色的东西说道，“是当地的特色菜，腌鳕鱼，就是鳕鱼。”听他说话的口气，就像那天早上他亲自为她们抓的鱼。

“看起来非常好。”领队说。

“我也觉得是。”他说。领队又摇了摇头。午餐结束时她很高兴。不过，这顿午餐很丰盛，当女士们回到会议室时，卡多扎在他的出租车里睡了个午觉。

两周之后，古巴女代表团抵达卢班戈参加妇女卫生大会。第一天早上，当她们走进酒店时，一个有趣的小个子男人过来迎接她们，脸上挂着灿烂的笑容。

“早上好，先生们。我是卡多扎，随时为您服务！”

他开出租车赚不了多少钱，但卡多扎当然知道怎样得到一顿免费的午餐。

A Free Lunch

By Jake Allsop

"Good morning, gentlemen. I am Cardosa, at your service!"

The group he was addressing were all women, but that did not bother Cardosa. He was proud of the English he had learned as a youngster. He spoke rapidly, smiling all the time as he did so. Unfortunately, he rarely understood what was said to him, but this did not bother him, either.

The women stared to him, not sure if he was an official or a madman.

"Welcome to Lubango. Welcome to the Great Hotel. Anything you want, ask Cardosa!"

The leader of the group decided he must be an official. "We are here for the conference, Comrade er..."

"Cardosa. C-A-R-D-O-S-A. I am an Angolan citizen. Welcome!"

She looked at him. He was clearly a European, probably one of those Portuguese who had stayed on after Independence. "We are here for the conference."

"Ah yes, a beautiful country," said Cardosa with another broad smile.

The women were from North Korea and weren't confident of their English. They didn't know if they had not understood him, or if he did not understand them.

"North Korea," said the leader uncertainly. "We have come for the Trade Union Congress."

Cardosa smiled again. He recognized the word "congress"; it was almost the same word in Portuguese. "Ah yes, the Congress! Please follow me, gentlemen."

The women looked at each other and then at Cardosa. He spread his arms out. "Do not worry! I know the way. I will take you the conference room." he led the way and the women, having no better alternative, followed him. He kept up a conversation over his shoulder as he walked. "Pleased to meet you. How are you? Anything you need? A taxi, cigarettes, eat, drink... just ask Cardosa."

"We are the North Korea delegation," the leader said. "Who are you?"

"I am very well," replied Cardosa.

"Are you our guide?"

He looked at his watch. It no longer worked, but it looked good on his wrist. "Eight-thirty!" He said confidently. The leader looked at her colleagues and shook her head.

He showed the delegates into the conference room and bowed low. "Goodbye. See you later, er, comrades."

When they came out at the end of the morning session, Cardosa waiting for them. "Good! You have talked, now you must eat. Follow me." As he led them towards the dining room, the leader tried again.

"Are you a government official, Comrade Cardosa?"

"Very good. Yes, the food here is very good. You will enjoy it!"

He sat next to the leader at the long dining-table which had been laid specially for them.

"This," he said, holding up something grey on the end of his fork, "is a local specialty, bacalhau. Codfish." He spoke as if he had personally caught it that morning just for them.

"It looks very good," said the leader.

"I do, too," he said. The leader shook her head again. She was glad when the lunch as over. It was a good lunch, though, and Cardosa went for a sleep in his taxi when the women went back to their conference.

A couple of weeks later, a delegation of Cuban women arrived in Lubango for the Women's Health Congress. As they walked into the hotel on the first morning, a funny little man came to greet them, a big smile on his face.

"Good morning, gentlemen. I am Cardosa, at your service!"

His taxi business made very little money, but Cardosa certainly knew how to get a free lunch.

吧唧，吧唧

在纽约城市中心一个条件不太好的公寓里住着一个名叫哈罗德·霍华德的人。他是个年轻人，也就25岁左右，他怕蟑螂怕得要死。嗯，假如你去过纽约，在一个萧条的旅馆里长期居住或者临时居住过，你就会知道那里的壁虎有多少，真是数不胜数！

霍华德刚下班回家，想稍稍放松一下。他只想捧着一碗冰激凌，坐下来看看报纸。他开始在又脏又乱的柜子搜，头探进去找碗和勺子。他找到了碗，拿出冰激凌，打开抽屉拿勺子，结果意想不到的事发生啦！！抽屉里跳出一只浑身湿漉漉的硕大蟑螂。他一蹦20英尺高，一把从抽屉里抓了一个勺子，一屁股坐下，让自己镇静镇静。“上帝啊，求你除掉蟑螂吧！”他喊道，这时，另一只蟑螂在他的两脚之间爬了过去，他的心跳都变慢了。“我总会找到摆脱它们的法子。”就在这时，当他吃着冰激凌阅读报纸上的广告时，一个专门广告引起了他的注意。“有蟑螂？我们有解决办法！今天到山姆宠物俱乐部去，获取蟑螂的天然捕食者——壁虎！”

“世界上有什么？”霍华德想着。他接着往下读：“没错！壁虎！按照下面的指示，获取你自己的活蟑螂消除器！然后咨询我们和蔼可亲的员工如何饲养壁虎和怎么除掉蟑螂。”“你说得对，壁虎很可能在我睡觉的时候把我吃掉。”他说，与此同时，另一只蟑螂在地板上跑来跑去。他感到恶心。他认为值得一试，所以第二天他就按照广告上的指示奔赴宠物店。

他问起壁虎，工作人员告诉他如何饲养壁虎，以及壁虎的价格，很快，他就带着自己的壁虎开车回家了。“太好了，”他想，“很快就有一个小家伙在我家里溜达了。”

他回到家里，就像店里的女导购告诉他要做的那样，把壁虎放了出来。他看见壁虎看到距离最近的蟑螂后立刻紧随其后钻进了冰箱下面。“嗯，至少他在尽职尽责。”他听到巨大的吧唧吧唧的声音以后说：“这是壁虎吞咽时发出的声音。”

日子一天天过去，霍华德看到蟑螂越来越少了。他不喜欢壁虎在家里跑来跑去，但是，是要一只壁虎，还是要一千只蟑螂呢？他耸耸肩，尽量忍着。然而，他还是做了一件事，就是在睡觉前关上门。但是不论他把门关得多么严实，壁虎总能想方设法进入他的房间。

一天下班以后，他正在吃晚饭的时候，看见壁虎在冰箱底下追赶屋子里最后那批蟑螂中的一只。他看见蟑螂快速从冰箱下面跑过去，壁虎远远地在后面追，挣扎着从冰箱下面挤过去。这时哈罗德才意识到，壁虎长得越来越大了。那天晚上，他竭尽全力把壁虎赶出他的房间。他沉沉地睡去了。

次日清晨，警察们都发现了床上的一个看上去像血的小污点。那天早上，一位忧心忡忡的邻居听到一声微弱的、似有似无的尖叫声和挥之不去的“吧唧、吧唧”声，他们满屋四处搜寻哈罗德，但是大家都一无所获：没有哈罗德，没有壁虎，没有蟑螂，什么也没有。他们大惑不解，狐疑地离开了那所房子，想着还能不能再见到哈罗德了。他们唯一没有检查过的地方是床底下，壁虎在那里，和以前一样大，然而这次终于吃饱了。

GECKO, GECKO

In downtown New York, at a somewhat trashy apartment, there lived a man named Harold Howard. He was a young man, in his mid-twenties, and had a terrible fear of cockcroaches. Well if you've been to New York, and maybe live or stayed in a rundown hotel, you know how many cockroaches there are. Too many to count!

Howard had just come home from work and was looking for a bit of relaxation. All he wanted to do was get a bowl of ice cream, sit down and read the newspaper. He started raiding the messy cabinets and sink to look for a bowl and a spoon. He found the bowl, got out the ice cream and opened a drawer to get the spoon when, Surprise!! Out jumps a big juicy cockroach. After jumping twenty feet in the air and grabbing a spoon out of the drawer, he sat down to calm himself. "God forsaken roaches!" he yelled, while slowing his heartbeat, just as another cockroach crawled between his feet. "There's got to be something I can do to get rid of them." Just then, as he was getting his ice cream and reading ads in the paper, one specific ad caught his eye. "Got Roaches?

We have a solution! Come down to Sam's Pet Club today and get yourself the natural predator of the roaches, a Gecko! "

"What in the world?" Howard thought. He read on: "That's right! A gecko! Follow the directions below to get your very own live cockroach eliminator! Then ask our friendly staff how to care for and what to do to get rid of your cockroaches." "Ya right. That gecko will probably eat me while I sleep." He said as yet another roach scuttled across the floor. He felt sick. He thought it was worth a try, so the very next day he followed the directions on the ad to the pet store.

He asked about the geckos and the staff told him what to do with a gecko and how much they were and, soon enough, he was driving home with his very own gecko. "Great," he thought, "yet another little critter that is going to be loitering around in my house."

He got home and did just as the woman at the store told him to do, and let the gecko go. He saw the gecko run under the refrigerator after the nearest cockroach it saw. "Well, at least he is doing his job." He said after he heard the loud "GECKO, GECKO", sound that geckos make when they swallow.

Days went by, and Howard saw fewer and fewer roaches. He didn't like the gecko running around his house all the time, but what's one gecko to a thousand roaches? He shrugged it off, and tried to suck it up. One thing he did do, however, was close the door before he went to bed. But no matter what he did, somehow the lizard always got into his room.

One day after work, he was getting some dinner when he saw the gecko chase one of the last cockroaches on the house under the refrigerator. He saw the cockroach scurry under it with the gecko far behind struggling to go under. That's when Harold realized. It was getting bigger. That night he did everything he could to keep the Gecko out of his room. He fell into a deep sleep.

All the police found the next morning was a small stain on the bed that looked like blood. They searched everywhere in the house for Harold after a worried neighbor heard a slight scream and a haunting "GECKO, GECKO", that morning, but no one could find anything. No Harold, No Gecko, No cockroaches, nothing. They left that house confused and wondering, never to see Harold again. The only place they didn't check was under the bed, where the gecko was-big as ever, and full at last.

抱抱先生

人们常常会问我这么大的女孩："你长大后想干什么？"我这么大的女孩总是回答，想成为公主、医生或者艺术家。

可是当人们问我的时候，我却兴高采烈地回答他们："当一个侦探！"

我现在可以见证了，侦探达西，街区里最棒的六岁侦探！

一个炎热的夏日午后，我坐在我的树屋里，在那里我处理自己的全部侦探事务。我有一段时间没有要处理的任何案件了，所以我正需要有人来告诉我，他们有一个谜团要我去解开呢。

果然，我听到有人爬上了通向我树屋的梯子，很可能是个新客户。

原来是三岁的"可爱的阿迪"，住在这条街上。她今天不像她平时那样活泼，看起来很沮丧。此外，她通常随身携带她的毛绒兔子——抱抱先生。现在，阿迪却没有带。

"达西！我的抱抱先生被绑架了！你得帮帮我！"

她说绑架？嗯，我是解决这个谜团的最佳人选。

"你最后一次见到他在哪里？"我问道。"上次见到抱抱先生时，他和谁在一起？"

阿迪想了一会儿。"几个小时前，我们和一些朋友在操场上开茶会。"她低声告诉我。"我和抱抱先生滑滑梯，却把他给掉下去了。当我去捡他时，他却不见啦！”

从这个声音判断，抱抱先生好像被阿迪的一个所谓的“朋友”绑架了。

“你跟哪些朋友一起去的？”我问道，我也知道会有很多朋友，大家都知道“可爱阿迪”爱交朋友。

阿迪扳着指头数朋友，回答说：“坎迪·坎普瑞舍思、碧翠丝·布鲁、费莉西蒂·范西，还有哈丽特·黑尔。”我从我坐的椅子上站起来，告诉阿迪：“你可以把你的朋友带到这里来吗？”

阿迪点点头，慌慌张张地跑去找她的朋友。

“别担心，阿迪，我会揭开这个谜底的。”阿迪从树屋的楼梯下到下面的草地上时，我向我的客户保证。

15 分钟以后，阿迪带她的朋友们一同回来了。

我们六个人都坐在我的树屋里，她们都坐在我面前。（除了阿迪，她是坐在我旁边的。）

为了听起来更专业，我开篇这样说道：“你一定想知道为什么我今天把你们都带到这里来。我肯定你们都认识抱抱先生，阿迪的绒毛兔子。”

坎迪、碧翠丝、费莉西蒂和哈丽特都缓缓地点了点头。

“好吧。”我继续说。“你们有谁知道抱抱先生今天早些时候被绑架了吗？基于我仔细的观察，你们四人中有一个人应该对这起绑架负责。”

四个女孩面面相觑，大惑不解。绑架者真的会在她们中间吗？

“坎迪。”我说，一个棕色辫子的女孩转向我。她穿着打了补丁的背带裤，里面穿了一件白衬衫。“坎迪，绑架发生时你在干什么？”

“那要看具体时间了。”坎迪羞怯地回答。“抱抱先生什么时候被绑架的？”

我没有回答那个问题。我怀疑是坎迪干的，因为她没有努力拿出一个现成的答案来。我从来没说过案发的具体时间，所以坎迪没办法知道抱抱先生是什么时候被绑架的。但是，她只是装作自己没有线索。

下一个女孩穿了一身蓝。碧翠丝蓝。“碧翠丝，你最后一次见到抱抱先生是在哪里？”

“在野餐篮子里，当时我和其他人在一起。我们去操场上玩，我回来就再没看见他。”碧翠丝立刻回答道。

“就跟真的似的。”我大声说出自己的想法，然后继续审问下一个嫌疑人。

下一个女孩脖子上戴了一条货真价实的珍珠项链，穿了一套华丽的衣服。“好吧，继续吧。我不是一整天都有空的，你也知道。”费莉西蒂一本正经地说道。

我被费莉西蒂粗鲁的话惹恼了。我问她：“你有一屋子稀有动物的毛绒玩具，对吧？”

费莉西蒂点了点头。

“抱抱先生被认为是罕见的毛绒动物。你一直想要抱抱先生吧？”我盯着她的眼睛问她。

“是的，我曾经想要过抱抱先生，”费莉西蒂回答道，这次的态度没有上次那么粗鲁了，“但我绝不会把他从阿迪手里夺走，她那么爱他。”

费莉西蒂很可能就是那个绑匪。也许她说阿迪爱抱抱先生只是为了让自己看起来更无辜。另外，她曾经想要过抱抱先生。

这让我想起了最后一个女孩，哈丽特·黑尔，就凭她的名字，看着她的衣服，我可以看出她喜欢兔子。她的衬衫上印满了兔子，她还戴了一条兔子手镯。

“哈丽特，你看起来很喜欢兔子。”我告诉她。但是哈丽特已经知道了。“阿迪有抱抱先生，你嫉妒过吗？”

“当我第一次遇见阿迪的时候，我是妒忌过，”哈丽特诚实地回答，“但去年圣诞节我得到了抱抱夫人，所以我不再嫉妒了。”

哈丽特看起来也像个嫌疑人。她说她不嫉妒，不是她一点儿也不嫉妒。而且，她也可能把抱抱先生带给她的洋娃娃——抱抱夫人，给抱抱夫人找个伴儿。

我把那些嫌疑人想了几分钟，然后才明白是谁带走了抱抱先生。

“阿迪，”我转向我的客户，开了口，“我知道是谁带走了他。”

阿迪俯身问道：“是谁？是谁带走了抱抱先生？”

坎迪、碧翠丝、费莉西蒂和哈丽特全都靠拢过来，仿佛她们在等着听一个篝火旁的故事结局。“耶！凶手吗？”碧翠丝公主问道。

“我只需要知道一件事，阿迪。你今天玩过沙或泥之类的东西吗？”我问道，心里期待她会说是的。如果她玩过，我就知道谁拿了抱抱先生了。

阿迪点点头，回答说：“是的，但是我看不出这和任何事情有什么关系！”

停顿了一秒钟以后，我告诉阿迪：“我有一个好消息，也有一个坏消息要告诉你。好消息是带走抱抱先生的人不在你的朋友中间。”

每个人，包括阿迪，都松了一口气。“好！我希望我不会被诬告为导致抱抱先生失踪的怪物！”费莉西蒂大声叫道，语气仍然是她那一本正经的语气。

“那么，谁把抱抱先生带走了？”阿迪问道，她现在有点儿糊涂了。我猜得出她很困惑，因为所有的嫌疑人都是无辜的，没人可审了。

我低声回答：“恐怕史上头号通缉犯已经把抱抱先生抓走了……邪恶的洗衣机！”

所有的女孩都呼吸急促起来。“你是说，抱抱先生要被洗了吗？”坎迪大声喊道，吓坏了。

“太可怕了！”费莉西蒂喊道。

哈丽特站起来，宣布说：“好吧，我们必须救他！我们必须把抱抱先生从邪恶的洗衣机里救出来！”坎迪、碧翠丝、费莉西蒂和哈丽特大声叫着表示同意，阿迪忧心忡忡地问：“达西，你确定现在还不晚吗？”

我耸了耸肩。“我不知道，因为每个人的邪恶洗衣机都不一样。我们只能尽快去看看他是否安全！”

阿迪抓起我树屋角落里的玩具枪，喊道：“快点儿，姑娘们！拿起你的战斗装备，我们去救抱抱先生吧！”

五个女孩迅速顺着梯子爬到草地上，开始飞奔。“等等！”我在树屋的门口大声喊道。

他们都停下来向我转过身来。“对付邪恶的洗衣机，你不能只用玩具枪！你必须更强大才行！回来吧，我借给你几件应景的衣服！”

女孩子们从我的衣柜里扯出几件衣服，套在她们平时的衣服上，形成了奇特的服装组合。然后，她们转过身来面对我。

阿迪穿了一件警服，戴着头带，看起来像长了兔耳朵。“我是一名警察！”她急切地喊道。“我戴着头带来展示我的兔子精神！”

坎迪穿了一套奇特的组合。她脸上戴了一个熊猫面具，头上戴着一顶皇冠，身披一件粉红色的超级英雄斗篷。“多好，多好！”坎迪唱了起来。“我是熊猫大力公主！”

与此同时，碧翠丝转过身来，头戴蓝色的假发，也身披着一件蓝色的超级英雄斗篷。斗篷后面有一对翅膀，那是我打扮成仙女过万圣节的时候用过的。“我是公主，但我是熊猫大力公主值得信赖的伙伴蓝色知更鸟！”碧翠丝宣布。

费莉西蒂穿着骑士服，告诉我们：“好吧，这套不像做公主那么伟大，但我是穿着闪亮盔甲的骑士！”（我没有勇气告诉她那是我哥哥的服装。）

哈丽特最后一个转过身来，戴着一只看起来像兔子的耳朵，说：“我是兔子！”

“现在我们去救抱抱先生吧！”阿迪喊道。

我们都很快离开了树屋，跑到了阿迪的家里。除了坎迪，她被我用车拉着，看起来像在飞。

阿迪家的一扇门没有锁，所以我们都破门而入，跟着阿迪去了邪恶洗衣机的窝——洗衣房。

我们很快找到了洗衣房，里面放着邪恶的洗衣机，但是里面黑洞洞的。

“我要把灯打开！”碧翠丝边喊边拍着电灯开关。

现在我们看到抱抱先生坐在洗衣机盖上，好像依旧准备好，就要被洗了似的，大家都气喘吁吁起来。

“我们会救你的，抱抱先生！”哈丽特大声喊道。

阿迪拿着我的玩具枪，所以她射出一颗吸盘子弹，打中了邪恶洗衣机的中部。吸盘子弹被卡在了洗衣机上，阿迪得意扬扬地喊道：“我打中了！”

因为阿迪个子矮，够不着抱抱先生，我小心翼翼地抓住了抱抱先生，说实话，他也确实该洗澡了，然后把他还给了阿迪。

“我们救了你，抱抱先生！”阿迪高兴地尖叫着，把抱抱先生从我手里接过来跟他拥抱了一下。

“抱抱先生，谢谢达西，是他帮助我们找到了你！”阿迪告诉她的娃娃。然后让他转过身来，面对着我。

“谢谢！”阿迪表示感谢，装作是抱抱先生说的话。

我和阿迪一起玩着，告诉抱抱先生：“不客气，抱抱先生。谢谢你终于给我提供了一个好的案例。”

“那么，这是侦探达西处理的又一个案子吧？”哈丽特问道。

“是的，哈丽特。”我回答。“达西侦探已经破案了！”

Mr. Snuggles

People may ask other girls my age, " What do you want to be when you grow up?" The girls my age always answer, a princess, a doctor, or an artist.

But when people ask me, I cheerfully answer them, "A detective!"

I can see it now, Darcy the Detective, the greatest 6-year-old detective on the block!

One scorching sunny summer afternoon, I sat in my tree house, where I do all my detective business. I haven't had any cases to solve for a while, so I just needed someone to come and tell me that they have a mystery for me to solve.

And sure enough, I heard someone climbing up the ladder to my tree house most likely a new client.

It was Addy Adorable, the three-year-old down the street. Unlike her usual bubbly self, she looked upset. Also, she normally carries around her stuffed bunny, Mr Snuggles. Now, Addy didn't have Mr. Snuggles with her.

"Darcy! My Mr. Snuggles has been kidnapped! You've got to

help me!"

A kidnapping, she says? Well, I'm the best person to solve this mystery.

"Where was the last place you saw him?" I asked. "And who was with Mr. Snuggles when you last saw him?"

Addy thought for a moment. "We were having a tea party at the play ground just a few hours ago with some friends," she told me in a hushed tone. "I slid down the slide with Mr. Snuggles, but dropped him. When I went to go pick him up, he was gone!"

From the sound of this, it sounded like Mr. Snuggles was kidnapped by one of Addy's so-called "friends".

"Which of your friends came with you?" I asked, knowing that there would be a lot. Addy Adorable was known for making friends easily.

Counting her friends off her fingers, Addy answered, "Candy Capricious, Beatrice Blue, Felicity Fancy, and Harriet Hare." Standing up from a chair I was sitting on, I told Addy, "Do you think you can bring your friends here?"

Addy nodded, and scampered to go find her friends.

"Don't you worry, Addy, I'll get to the bottom of this mystery," I assured my client before she climbed down the ladder to the grass.

It took fifteen minutes for Addy Adorable to come back with her friends.

All six of us fit into my wooden tree house, and they all sat to face me. (Except for Addy, who sat next to me.)

Wanting to sound professional, I started, " You must be wondering why I've brought you all here today. I'm sure you all know Mr. Snuggles, Addy's stuffed rabbit."

Candy, Beatrice, Felicity, and Harriet all nodded slowly.

"Well, " I continued. "Were any of you aware that Mr. Snuggles was kidnapped earlier today? Based on my careful observations. one of you four are responsible for the kidnapping."

The four girls looked at each other, confused. Could a kidnapper really be among them?

"Candy," I addressed, and a girl with brown pigtails turned to me. She had patched overalls on, and a white shirt underneath. "Candy, what were you doing at the time of the kidnapping?"

"That depends," Candy sheepishly replied. "When was Mr. Snuggles kidnapped?"

I left that question alone. I doubted that it would've been Candy, since she didn't try to come up with an answer. I never said what time it was at, so there was no way for Candy to know when Mr. Snuggles was kidnapped. But, she could just be acting like she was clueless.

The next girl had everything blue on. Beatrice Blue. "Beatrice, where was Mr. Snuggles when you last saw him?"

"I was at the picnic blanket with everyone else. I didn't

see him after we went to go play on the playground," Beatrice immediately answered.

"Likely story," I thought out loud, going to the next suspect.

The next girl wore a necklace of real pearls around her neck, and wore a fancy outfit. Felicity Fancy. "Okay, get on with it. I don't have all day, you know," Felicity remarked, all prim and proper.

Annoyed by Felicity's rude remark. I asked her. "You have room of rare stuffed animals, right?"

Felicity nodded.

"Mr. Snuggles is considered rare stuffed animal. Have you always wanted Mr. Snuggles?" I asked, looking her straight in the eyes.

"Yes, I have wanted Mr. Snuggles," Felicity answered, a bit less rude this time, "But I would never take him from Addy. She loves him so much."

Felicity was a likely kidnapper. Maybe she just said that she loves Mr. Snuggles just so it seems like she's innocent. Plus, she has wanted Mr. Snuggles.

That brought me to the last girl, Harriet Hare, Just by her name, and looking at her clothes, I could tell that she liked bunnies. Her shirt was covered with bunnies, and she had a rabbit bracelet.

"Harriet, you seem to like bunnies," I told her, but Harriet already knew that. "Have you ever been jealous of Addy's possession of Mr. Snuggles?"

"When I first met Addy, yes," Harriet honestly answered. "But I got Mrs. Snuggles last Christmas, so I'm not as jealous anymore."

Harriet also seemed like a suspicious suspect. She said that she wasn't as jealous, not that she's not jealous at all. Also, she could have taken Mr. Snuggles to give her doll, Mrs. Snuggles, a partner.

I thought about the suspects for a few minutes, before I realized something that made it clear who took Mr. Snuggle.

"Addy," I started, turning toward my client. "I know who took Mr. Snuggles."

Addy leaned in and asked, "Who? Who took Mr. Snuggles?"

Candy, Beatrice, Felicity, and Harriet all scooted closer, as if they were waiting to hear the end of a campfire story. "Yeah! Who dunnit?" Beatrice asked.

"I just need to know one thing, Addy. Did you play in something like sand or dirt before today?" I asked, hoping she would say yes. If she did, I knew who took Mr. Snuggles.

Addy nodded and answered, "Yes, but I don't see how that has to do with anything!"

Pausing for a second. I told Addy, "Well, I have good news and I have bad news for you. The good news is that none of your friends is the person who took Mr. Snuggles."

Everyone, including Addy, gave a sigh of relief. "Good! I was hoping that I wouldn't be falsely accused of the monstrosity of Mr. Snuggles disappearance!" Felicity exclaimed, still in her prim and proper tone.

"Well then, who did take Mr. Snuggles?" Addy asked, a little confused now. I guess she was confused because all the suspects were innocent, leaving no one to interrogate.

In a hushed voice, I answered, "I'm afraid Mr. Snuggles has been taken by the most wanted crook of all time... the wicked washing machine!"

All the girls gasped. "You mean, Mr. Snuggles is going to be cleaned?!" Candy shouted, terrified.

"How dreadful!" Felicity cried.

Harriet stood up and declared, "Well, we have to save him! We have to save Mr. Snuggles from the wicked washing machine!" Candy, Beatrice, and Felicity yelled in agreement, and Addy worriedly asked, "Darcy, are you sure it's not too late?"

I shrugged. "I don't know, because everyone's wicked washing machine is different. We just have to go and see if he's safe!"

Addy grabbed the toy gun in the corner of my tree-house and yelled, "Come on, girls! Grab your battle gear, and let's go save Mr. Snuggles!"

The five girls quickly climbed down the ladder leading to the grass, and began to dash away. "Wait!" I shouted from the door of my tree-house.

They all stopped and turned to me. "You can't face a wicked washing machine with just a toy gun! You have to be stronger than it! Come back and I'll let you borrow a couple of the clothes I wear for times like these!"

After the girls threw multiple clothes out of my dress-up box, and put strange combinations of costumes over their regular clothes, they turned around to face me.

Addy had a police shirt on with a headband that made it look like you had bunny ears. "I'm a policewoman!" she eagerly shouted. "And I'm showing my bunny spirit with the headband!"

Candy had a stranger combination. She had a panda mask, a crown on her head, and a pink superhero cape. "Duuuh-duh-duuuuuuuuuuh!" Candy sang. "I'm Princess Power Panda!"

Beatrice tuned around at the same time with a blue wig, and another superhero cape that was blue. Behind the cape was a pair of wings from the time when I dressed up as a fairy for Halloween. "And I'm Princess, but I'm Princess Power Panda's trusty sidekick Bluebird!" Beatrice announced.

Felicity had a knight costume on, and told us, "Well, it's not as great as being a princess, but I'm a knight in shining armor!" (I didn't have the guts to tell her that it was my brother's costume.)

Harriet turned around last with an on-ear that looked like a bunny and said, "I'm a bunny!"

“Now let’s go rescue Mr. Snuggles!” Addy shouted.

All of us quickly left the tree-house, and ran to Addy’s house. Except for Candy, who was being pulled in a wagon by me to make it look like she was flying.

One of the doors to Addy’s house was unlocked, so we all went through the door and followed Addy to the wicked washing machine’s lair...the laundry room.

We quickly found the Laundry room, with the wicked washing machine sitting inside the room but in the dark.

“I’ll light the room up!” Beatrice shouted as she licked the light-switch.

Everyone gasped when we now saw that Mr. Snuggles was sitting on top of the washing machine, like he was getting ready to be cleaned.

“We’ll save you, Mr. Snuggles!” Harriet shouted.

Addy had my toy gun, so she shot one of the suction-cup bullets, hitting the wicked washing machine on the middle. The suction-cup bullet stuck, and Addy victoriously yelled, “I’m got him!”

Since Addy couldn’t reach Mr. Snuggles from the height he was at, I gingerly took Mr. Snuggles, who honestly did need a bath, and gave him back to Addy.

“We saved you, Mr. Snuggles!” Addy joyfully screeched as she took Mr. Snuggles from me and gave him a huge hug.

"Mr. Snuggles, say thank you to Darcy for helping us find you!" Addy told her doll. Turning him around so he faced me.

"Thank you!" Addy thanked. Trying to make it look like Mr. Snuggles was the one who was talking.

Playing along with Addy, I told "Mr. Snuggles", "You're very welcome, Mr. snuggles. Thank you for finally giving me a good case."

"So, another case solved for Darcy the Detective?" Harriet asked.

"That's right, Harriet," I replied. "Darcy the Detective has cracked the case!"

纯肉制造

［美国］泰里·比森

“他们是用肉做的。”

“肉？”

“是肉。他们是用肉做的。”

“肉？”

“根本就不需要怀疑，是我们从星球的几个不同的地方搜集来的，然后带回我们的侦察船上，一路检测，证明他们是纯肉。”

“这不可能，那无线电信号怎么解释？发给星星的信息呢？”

“他们用无线电波说话，但信号并非来自他们。这些信号来自机器。”

“谁造的机器？这才是我们想联系的人。”

“他们造的机器。这就是我想告诉你的。肉制造了机器。”

“这太荒谬了。肉怎么制造机器？你这是要我相信存在有知觉的肉。”

“我不是在请教你，我是在告诉你。这些生物是该领域中唯一有知觉的物种，他们是用肉制造出来的。”

“也许他们很像外星人俄浮雷，你知道，就是那种以碳元素为基础的智能生物，这种生物经历了一个肉质阶段。”

“不对，他们生于肉，死于肉。我们研究了他们的寿命周期，没花多长时间。你知道肉的寿命有多长吗？”

“饶了我吧。好吧，也许他们只是个别肉。你知道，就像韦德利一样。里面有电子浆大脑的肉头。”

“不行。我们想到了这一点，因为他们像韦德利一样有肉头。可我告诉过你，我们检测过他们。他们一路吃肉。”

“没有大脑？”

“哦，有一个大脑还行，只不过恰好这个大脑是肉制造的！这就是我一直想告诉你的。”

“那么……什么器官负责思考？”

“你还没明白，是吗？我告诉你的，你根本就没听。大脑负责思考，肉负责思考。”

“会思考的肉！你要我相信存在会思考的肉！”

“是的，会思考的肉！有意识的肉！有爱心的肉，有梦想的肉，肉是重点！你开始明白了吗？还是我必须从头开始？”

“天哪！那么你是认真的。他们是肉制造出来的。”

“谢谢。你终于明白了。对。他们确实是用肉制造的。他们一直在试图与我们取得联系，已经快一百年了。”

“天哪，那么这肉脑袋里面想什么呢？”

“首先他想和我们谈谈。然后我推测他想要探索宇宙，接触其他感觉，交流思想和信息，那些常见的。”

“我们应该和肉说说话。”

“这个想法好。这就是他们通过无线电发送的信息：‘你好。那里有人吗？有人在家吗？’诸如此类。”

“那么，他们是真的会说话。他们会使用词汇、观念、概念？”

“哦，是的。只是他们是用肉做到的。”

“我以为你刚才跟我说他们用的是无线电。”

“他们用的的确是无线电，但是你认为无线电里能有什么？肉发出的声音。你知道当你拍打或拍打肉的时候会发出声音吧？他们通过拍打肉说话。他们甚至可以通过肉内部的空隙喷气唱歌呢。”

“天哪。会唱歌的肉。这些也太过分啦。那么，你有什么建议？”

“官方的还是非正式的？”

“两种都要。”

“从官方角度，我们要求在没有偏见、恐惧或偏爱的前提下，接触、欢迎和录入宇宙象限中任何已经有意识的物种或众生。从非正式的角度，我建议我们删除记录，把这件事忘个一干二净。”

“我巴不得你这么说呢。”

“这听起来似乎很苛刻，但有一个限度。我们真的想与肉类接触吗？”

“我百分之百同意。有什么好说的？‘喂，肉，过得怎么样？’可这么说有用吗？我们在这里要应付多少行星？”

“只有一个。他们可以乘坐特殊的肉制容器到其他星球飞行，但是他们不能在其他星球上生存。作为肉类，他们只能在C空间飞行。这就把他们的速度限制在光速以内了，使他们可能发出的接触信号相当微弱，实际上是无穷小。”

“所以我们只是假装宇宙中没有人在家。”

“就是这样。”

“残忍。可你自己说的，谁想见肉？那些上过我们船的人，是你探测到的？你肯定他们不会记得了吗？”

“如果他们说记得，他们会被认为是疯子。我们进入他们的大脑，抚平他们的肉，这样我们就只不过是他们的一场梦罢了。”

“关于肉的梦！好奇怪，好合适啊，我们竟成了肉的梦。”

“我们标明那个区域全是无人区。”

“好。同意，不论官方还是非正式的。结案。还有其他的吗？银河系那边还有有趣的生物吗？”

“有，一个羞羞答答然而甜美可人的氢核心集群智能在G445区第九颗星上。在两次银河旋转之前曾经联系过我们，希望再次修好。”

“他们总归会回来的。”

“为什么不呢？想象一下，一个人如果孤孤单单，宇宙会变得多么难以忍受，那种寒冷真是难以形容啊……”

They're Made out of Meat

By Terry Bisson

"They're made out of meat."

"Meat?"

"Meat. They're made out of meat."

"Meat?"

"There's no doubt about it. We picked up several from different parts of the planet, took them aboard our recon vessels, and probed them all the way through. They're completely meat."

"That's impossible. What about the radio signals? The messages to the stars?"

"They use the radio waves to talk, but the signals don't come from them. The signals come from machines."

"So who made the machines? That's who we want to contact."

"They made the machines. That's what I'm trying to tell you. Meat made the machines."

"That's ridiculous. How can meat make a machine? You're

asking me to believe in sentient meat."

"I'm not asking you, I'm telling you. These creatures are the only sentient race in that sector and they're made out of meat."

"Maybe they're like the orfolei. You know, a carbon-based intelligence that goes through a meat stage."

"Nope. They're born meat and they die meat. We studied them for several of their life spans, which didn't take long. Do you have any idea what's the life span of meat?"

"Spare me. Okay, maybe they're only part meat. You know, like the weddilei. A meat head with an electron plasma brain inside."

"Nope. We thought of that, since they do have meat heads, like the weddilei. But I told you, we probed them. They're meat all the way through."

"No brain?"

"Oh, there's a brain all right. It's just that the brain is made out of meat! That's what I've been trying to tell you. "

"So...what does the thinking?"

"You're not understanding, are you? You're refusing to deal with what I'm telling you. The brain does the thinking. The meat."

"Thinking meat! You're asking me to believe in thinking meat!"

"Yes, thinking meat! Conscious meat! Loving meat. Dreaming

meat. The meat is the whole deal! Are you beginning to get the picture or do I have to start all over?"

"Omigod. You're serious then. They're made out of meat."

"Thank you. Finally. Yes. They are indeed made out of meat. And they've been trying to get in touch with us for almost a hundred of their years."

"Omigod. So what does this meat have in mind?"

"First it wants to talk to us. Then I imagine it wants to explore the Universe, contact other sentiences, swap ideas and information. The usual."

"We're supposed to talk to meat."

"That's the idea. That's the message they're sending out by radio. 'Hello. Anyone out there. Anybody home.' That sort of thing."

"They actually do talk, then. They use words, ideas, concepts?"

"Oh, yes. Except they do it with meat."

"I thought you just told me they used radio."

"They do, but what do you think is on the radio? Meat sounds. You know how when you slap or flap meat, it makes a noise? They talk by flapping their meat at each other. They can even sing by squirting air through their meat."

"Omigod. Singing meat. This is altogether too much. So what do you advise?"

"Officially or unofficially?"

"Both."

"Officially, we are required to contact, welcome and log in any and all sentient races or multi beings in this quadrant of the Universe, without prejudice, fear or favor. Unofficially, I advise that we erase the records and forget the whole thing."

"I was hoping you would say that."

"It seems harsh, but there is a limit. Do we really want to make contact with meat?"

"I agree one hundred percent. What's there to say? 'Hello, meat. How's it going?' But will this work? How many planets are we dealing with here?"

"Just one. They can travel to other planets in special meat containers, but they can't live on them. And being meat, they can only travel through C space. Which limits them to the speed of light and makes the possibility of their ever making contact pretty slim. Infinitesimal, in fact."

"So we just pretend there's no one home in the Universe."

"That's it."

"Cruel. But you said it yourself, who wants to meet meat? And the ones who have been aboard our vessels, the ones you probed? You're sure they won't remember?"

"They'll be considered crackpots if they do. We went into their heads and smoothed out their meat so that we're just a dream to them."

"A dream to meat! How strangely appropriate, that we should be meat's dream."

"And we marked the entire sector unoccupied."

"Good. Agreed, officially and unofficially. Case closed. Any others? Anyone interesting on that side of the galaxy?"

"Yes, a rather shy but sweet hydrogen core cluster intelligence in a class nine star in G445 zone. Was in contact two galactic rotations ago, wants to be friendly again."

"They always come around."

"And why not? Imagine how unbearably, how unutterably cold the Universe would be if one were all alone..."

葬尸之地

［爱尔兰］肖恩·卡瓦纳

坟能有多浅？

他之前从来没有挖过坟。在炎热的沙漠里，他从沙土上挖出的那个洞看上去很深，但现在他把尸体推进去，突然觉得这个洞很浅。会不会有动物或者其他东西把尸体挖出来？或者这就是重点？只要埋得可以盖住尸体，但不需要挖得太深，那样的话，尸体腐烂需要太长时间。

这还真是电视里教得更好。他弯下腰，喝了口水杯的水。从车里拖尸体拖了100英尺已经够累了，他不想再把它拖回去。

头顶上有东西在叫唤。看上去是真的在叫。不是一只雄蜂。可能是一只鸟。没有人造的机器在记录他此时此刻的行为。

接着他突然想到：可能有其他人的尸体正好也埋在这里。或许他应该另找一个坟地再往深处挖挖？或许他会找到一具被“谋杀”的尸体，然后可以看看专业人士是怎么埋的？但是他已经汗流浃背，提醒他这是一个愚蠢的想法。他从小背包里拿出地图（指导他如何埋尸的），然后卷起来放到尸体的口袋里。地图上写着“跟尸体一起埋葬，不要烧掉”。它只是一张纸，用不了多久就会腐烂。

头顶上有鸟在盘旋。看上去情况不太好。

他站了起来。

平坦的沙漠泛着热光。对他来说已经够陌生的了，但是透过热空气的镜头，岩层和灌木丛显得更加奇特和遥远，这地方不适合他待。

“对不起了，伙计。”他边对尸体说着，边往尸体上铲了第一锹土。这足足花了40分钟，然后他把土踩实，最后填完了坟。他往坟上面踢了一些表土和石头，希望可以盖住不自然的长方形的轮廓。

现在时间太晚了。

一阵风吹来，接着就吹走了。沙漠是一个不断变化的地方。他考虑了一会儿，是不是应该对着这座没有标记的坟墓说几句话，但这似乎是不对的，而且他什么也不想说。

他走回车里，喝了口水杯的水。杯子是隔热的，但装在里面的凉水已经有点儿温了。

副驾座位上放着一本白色的书，上面写着：手册。正是因为这本书，他才会在这里。他拿起书翻到第一页。

注意事项（1）：尸体必须要埋在一个这死者的家人和朋友都不会发现的地方。（请参照分页式地图选择埋葬地点。）

在注意事项旁边有一个框，他在里面打了个对号然后把书扔回座位。上面写着“无缝人际交互协议”，字体夸张。下面用讽刺的语气写着：“如何做一个规范的克隆人？”这句话是现在埋在坑里的那个人写的，但是现在属于他了。他把书翻过来，然后驾车走了，回到了文明世界，回到了“认识”他的人身边。准备继续过那个被埋葬的人的生活。

Where the Bodies are Buried

By Sean Kavanagh

How shallow was a shallow grave?

He'd never dug one before. The hole before him, which he'd gouged out of the sandy soil in the heat of the desert looked deep, but now he'd pushed the man's body into it, suddenly it looked awfully shallow. Could animals or other things get down to the body? Or maybe that was the point? Just deep enough for cover, but not so deep that it took too long for the flesh to turn to corruption.

This was really something TV should have taught him better. He hunched down and drank from his water flask. Dragging the body the hundred feet from the car had been exhausting enough so he wasn't about to drag it back.

Something squawked overhead. It looked real. Not a drone. Maybe a bird. Nothing man-made that would record what he was doing.

Then an idea hit: there were bound to be other bodies buried out here. Maybe he should find another grave and dig down a little? Maybe he could find the body of a "whacked" guy and see how the professionals did it? A little river of sweat ran down his back, reminding him that it was a stupid idea. He took the map (which had instructed him where to bury the body) from his satchel and tucked it into the dead body's pocket. They'd written "bury with body, do not burn" on it. It was paper, so would decay quickly enough.

Overhead more of the birds were circling. That didn't look too good.

He stood up.

The desert plain shimmered with heat. It looked alien enough already, but through the lens of hot air, the rock formations and scrub seemed even more curious and distant. This wasn't a place for him.

"Sorry buddy," he said to the body and shovelled the first pan of dirt over it. It took forty minutes and plenty of foot stamping, but finally the grave was filled. He kicked some topsoil and rocks onto it, hoping to disguise its unnaturally rectangular outline. Maybe he should have dug something with a more organic shape.

Too late now.

A wind whipped up and then was gone. The desert was an ever changing place. For a moment he considered whether he should say some words over the unmarked grave, but it didn't seem right. And there was nothing he wanted to say.

He walked back to the car, drinking from the flask. It was insulated, but the cool water inside had started to turn tepid already.

On the passenger seat was a white book: The Manual. It was why he was out here in this place. He picked it up and opened it to page 1.

ITEM(1): The body of your predecessor must be disposed of in a location, such that the family and friends of the deceased will not detect it or have reason to detect it. (See detachable map for disposal suggestions for your location.)

There was a box next to the item line. He ticked it and threw the book back onto the seat. It landed title up: "Protocols for Seamless Human Interaction" it read in pompous type. Below it, sarcastically, was scribbled: "How to be a Good Clone." The handwriting belonged to the man in the ditch. The handwriting belonged to him now. He turned the book over and drove off, back to civilization, back to the people who "knew" him. Ready to continue the life of the buried man.

丢 心

说我拿把刀子剖开胸膛取出心脏一丢了之，这说起来容易，可是不幸的是，做起来却没那么容易。并非是我异于常人，不经常想这么做。不是的，情况并非如此，而是出乎我的意料。

事情发生在我分别跟一个男人吃过午饭，跟另一个男人喝过下午茶之后。跟我吃午饭的那个男人是我同居了（大约）四又十二分之七年的伴侣，他离开我另攀高枝的时候，我过了两年也许是三年半死不活的日子。我的心变成了一块石头，心已经不能够随身而动，觉得身上的其他器官都压在心上了。后来，我慢慢地、艰难地挣脱出来，因为我的千万心结都牵挂在我的初恋身上，尽管从另一个角度来看，他应该是我的第二个真爱（我的父亲应该是我的第一个真爱）或者第三个真爱（这中间应该插入我的哥哥）。

正如民歌里所唱的那样：

我这一生爱了三个人，

我爸、我哥，还有那个要了我命的人。

然而，如果从外部因素而非内部因素来看的话，他应该是我的第13个（大概是吧，我记不得了）真爱。不过这么看的话，就意味着对内在的感情因素的无视。在一个真爱与另一个真爱之间所发生的风流韵事和纠缠可能有十几个人，延续多少年，但是其实都不算数。

这样看待问题的话，可能会招致很多人的不快，因为我们都明白，一方认为不算数的，另一方却有可能认为是算数的。然而，要克服这一困难，并非易事，因为真爱是人生至要，或者说差不多是最重要的。我们中的大多数人都忙于对它的寻寻觅觅，即便在我们严肃地爱着某个人的时候，我们依然瞪着第八只眼看是否会邂逅某个陌生人而后证明这个陌生人更值得严肃对待。我们对此都完全没有异议：在我们寻觅真正的那一个的路上，我们都有权利去品尝、尝试、品味成千上万个对象。说在我们的圈子里，品尝和品味是人生的第二大活动，这并不过分。人生第一重要的是赚钱。换句话说，你若是对此认真起来的话，只要对方主动，你会跟每个人都上床，在找到真正的那一个之前，你会一直这样继续下去。

我离题了。我至今仍把跟我共进午餐的那个男人（我们就叫他A吧）视为我的初恋，尽管弗洛伊德的信徒坚持把我的父亲视为A，可能还把我的哥哥视为B，把我（真正的）初恋视为C。也不管那些人问我：那你的两个丈夫呢？你那些婚外情呢？这些人算什么？

他们？我从来就没有真正爱过他们，没有像爱A那样爱过他们。

我跟A吃了午餐。接着，十分偶然地与B喝了下午茶。我在这里说的B，指的是我的第二个真爱，而不是我的哥哥，也不是我在五岁至15岁之间爱上的那些小男孩。我们也许可以把15岁（倒没有什么特别的理由）视为“不归点”，而“不归点”这个词本身就是对世俗仲裁者的大胆反抗。

（按照我的算法）我在A和B之间还有许许多多风流韵事，或者说品尝，但是都不算数。我和B一拍即合，我们像炸弹一样爆炸，尽管过程没有像跟A那么简单，因为刚刚被A抛弃，我的心受伤了，红肿了，心生疑窦。此外，我与A的种种藕断丝连还未一一扯清。尽管如此，一时间，我与B如起火的老屋，继而转入悲哀，我的心再度负重，垂在肋下。

我肋下的若是石头一块，石头一块的话，

我倒可以把它掏出来，获得自由。

与A共进午餐，与B喝下午茶，耗尽我花样年华的十年光景（我没把期间的尝试、品尝算进去）。公平地讲，这平衡了所有的喜（多而浓烈）和所有的悲（哦，上帝，上帝）——从一个人漂泊到另一个人，亲热地又是谈这又是谈那的，与此同时我的心不过是在淡淡的回忆中挣扎，记忆之鱼在长长的、松松的钓线的另一端……

总而言之，很健康。

特别是，那天晚上我准备见C，或者说可能成为C的人。我不想刻意突出C，因为事实上我几乎不记得他长得什么样，人们是无法记得真爱之间出现的那些浅尝辄止、无关紧要的人的。然而，说到底，他有可能成为C，我们有可能一拍即合，而我的思想状态是（我们经常有这样的思想状态）：他有可能就是那一个。（我有意使用妇女杂志上的用词，用“那一个”，而不是“或许会认真对待”。）

于是，我就这样（我想要把所有细节和气氛都搞好）站在窗前，看着一条街道（说得确切些，是波特兰大道），心中想着，我从来都没有为跟A和B的恋爱经历后悔过（爱过失去过，总比从未爱过强），而我期待着与C共同度过一个晚上，这也不现实，因为毕竟A和B都曾经给我带来过令人难以置信的痛苦。那么，我为什么还要期待C？我应该以最快的速度逃才是。

我突然发觉自己对这一问题始终认识得不够准确。我的（我可以说我们的吗？）看法是我们应该在具备某种既合情又合理的综合素质的前提下，去寻觅ABCD，这样双方才能一拍即合，同时燃烧；换句话说，一个人漂浮在一盘水里，需要另一个人像一个摆渡人似的，把自己向他或者她摆过去。然而，其实情况根本不是这样。其实，每个人胁下都插着一根燃烧的长矛，等待别人给拔出来，而这像痛处和伤口一样，非常痛苦，其实根本等不到分担之人。

在这片刻的真实中，我把自己看得一清二楚：我站在窗前（三楼），把A和B抛在脑后。我是个相当迷人的女人，如果我可以这么说的话，我还是个成熟的女人，我也是第一个承认成熟是韶华将逝的可悲先兆。然而，我确凿无疑是一个风情万种的女人，因为年轻时这么多的尝试、浅斟（我差点儿写成“招式”“前任”）可以证实……我就站在那里，精挑细选过衣服，描过眉，点过朱唇，画过眼晕，全都是为了等待晚上可能的C。而在另一扇窗前站着C，俯瞰着（我想我并没有猜错）玛嘉丽街，擦过皮鞋，洗过澡，刮过胡子，面带微笑，魅力无限（我认为）。他在想，我会成为他的D（或者是A抑或是3或者是？或者是%，或者管他用什么代号呢）。我们都站着，当然在空间上是不同的，心理状态却是一致的——对于未来的不确定的愉快的期待。我们都把自己的心握在手里，两颗心都是粉粉的、颤颤的，准备迎接快乐和痛苦。我们打算把这些心像抛掷雪球或者板球一样（如何？）抛掷到对方的脸上，或者更确切地说像抛掷血淋淋的大伤口一样：“接住我的伤口。”此刻他或者她绝对想不到对方会说：接住我的伤口，请把我胁下的长矛拔出来。想不到，绝对想不到，人们只想祛除自己的伤痛。

我决定去打个电话，说，C！——你知道那个笑话开玩笑的人的笑话吧？说开玩笑的人懒得给开玩笑的人说笑话的内容，所以只说笑话1或者笑话2，大家相应地哄堂大笑，或者低声窃笑，或者咯咯地笑……这个游戏也可以反过来玩，那就是根据一个人的笑声的类型来对应没说出的笑话内容……嗯，C啊（我想象自己这么说），这个笑话对我们来说有启发：我们权且把这个笑话当真，把笑话的内容当成已经说过了。

我们不必去舔对方的伤口，我们把自己的心事留给自己。C 啊，你不妨脑补一下，你我站在各自的窗前，手里拿着颤颤的心，这画面真是荒谬透顶……

亲爱的读者，我此刻不得不放下电话，向你们致歉。我的左手手指推出了一个大大的、轻轻的、滑滑的东西——这种感觉难以形容，真的。我的手不大，而我的心在与 A 共进午餐与 B 喝过下午茶以及盼望 C 之后进入肿胀状态……尽管如此，我拼命伸开手指抓住这个大大的、轻轻的莫名其妙的东西，因此，我对 C 说道：请稍等。我低头一看，看到我的心，就在我的手里。

我只得挂掉电话。

首先，不费吹灰之力地得到一件曾经朝思暮想的东西，让人不免心生不快，这与经过千辛万苦得到不一样。碰巧得到一件想要的东西——不，这样没有乐趣，没有成就感。在跟一个可能成为 C 的人打虚拟电话时，在这样的尴尬时刻，却发现自己有一颗完整的心，准确地说，发现自己的心已经不在其位，摆脱了这个该死的东西，哎呀，真是气人。

再者，一颗刚从胸腔里拿出来的心是赤裸裸、活生生、血淋淋的，绝非最美的养眼之物。我不想继续说下去了。我很震惊，也确实很尴尬，这就是多年以来爱情和时光的消磨之物，若是我以往对此有所了解的话——唉，不说了。

我现在所面临的问题是怎么摆脱它。

你会说，很简单，扔进垃圾桶呗。

唉，我告诉你，我已经试过了。我看了看这个东西，几乎没羞死，然后向垃圾桶走去，我想把它从手上抖落下去，可是抖落不下去，粘住了。我的心就在那里，就在我的手上，大大的，红红的，血淋淋的，跳个不停。我该怎么办？我坐下来，点燃了一支香烟（用一只手点的，用两个膝盖夹着火柴），粘着心的那只手耷拉到椅子的一侧，这样血水就能滴进垃圾桶里。

若是我手里握着的是一块石头，一块石头，

我就可以把它从一棵树上扔过去……

抽完了烟，我小心翼翼地把包食物用的锡箔剥下来，给我的心做了一个套样的东西。这么做很有必要，也是势在必行。因为，第一，我的心在痛，说到底，四十多年以来，我的心一直被骨肉保护着，现在暴露在了空气里。第二，我不能让阿猫阿狗们进来看到。第三，我自己看得时间长了，也会满怀羞愧。而锡箔纸很管用，确实也够惹眼。它现在在我手里，看起来就像一个银光闪闪的球，有型又有款，我差点儿都觉得只有在另一只手上放上一个权杖才能对称平衡……不过，这东西概括起来只有一个字——俗，于是，我在裹着心的锡箔上裹了一条丝巾，这样感觉安全了些。现在面临的问题就是：先装作手受伤了，再想办法彻底摆脱这颗心，不能把手也锯掉。

与此同时，我打电话（是真打，不是打虚拟电话）给C，他现在永远也不会成为C了。我能够感觉到紧紧地粘在手上的心的每一次跳动和战栗，为拥有这种前所未有的美妙体验而如释重负。我跟他说了一个因为感冒不能赴约的笨拙的谎言。嗯，他恼羞成怒，却礼貌地掩饰着，就像我也会做的那样，开了句玩笑，话里略微带着刺，精挑细选了一句结束的话。然后，我坐了下来，思考我现在的处境。

我就坐在那里。

我该何去何从？

我就坐在那里。

我将把接下来四天所发生的事跳过去，因为凭良心讲，这非常必要，原因是我根本无法回忆一段段感情了。可惜了，因为我认为这是这个故事的关键。简单扼要地说就是：我拉上窗帘，从电话机上把听筒摘下来，把灯都打开，从银光闪闪的心上把丝巾解下来，然后打开锡箔，审视我的心。我要审视五分之二世纪的经历，可是，还没等我审视完第一夜，我就进入了难以描绘状态……

或许若是我拔出皮肤上的神经腺，

快速把一张红色的网拖进大海捕鱼……

到了第四天，我已经筋疲力尽。不论是依靠意念、意向或是意欲，我都无法撼动那颗心一丝一毫——恰恰相反，它不仅像块高温熬制的硬糖，而且实际上已经长在我的手掌和手指上了。

我再次用锡箔和丝巾把它包了起来，关了灯，拉上了百叶窗和窗帘。此时大约是上午十点，伦敦普普通通的一天，既不太冷也不太热，既不太晴也不太阴，既不太湿也不太干，街上算是有趣，却谈不上美丽，所以，我也没指望会看到什么吸引我注意力的景象，心中另有想法。

突然，我听到了笃笃笃的声音，这声音越来越大，越来越刺耳，越来越清晰，因此，在没有见到她的人之前，我就已经知道这是高跟鞋踏在人行道上的声音，尽管这也可以是锤子敲打石头的声音。她在我窗户对面的人行道上疾步前行，鞋跟重重地踏在人行道上，笃笃作响的声音吞没了这条街上的一切噪声。她走到波特兰大道拐角处的时候，两只伦敦的鸽子呈对角线向下俯冲，像两颗瞄准她想要她的命的子弹。一看到她，两个鸽子随即呈直角一飞冲天。她转过街角。这一切发生在一瞬间，可是，要把这些写下来却需要时间：那个女人体内的力量通过高跟鞋敲打着人行道，然后她在街角拐了一个正角；两只鸽子又在她身旁来了个急转弯，在无所依傍的空中迅速俯冲着横穿过去。一切都没什么，当然，没什么——她在街上走着，高跟鞋笃笃地响着，两只鸽子落在我的窗台上，开始咕咕地叫了起来。一切都成了过往云烟，都消失无痕了，那声音与动作奇妙地琴瑟相和、丝丝入扣，可是的确曾经发生过，让我欣喜若狂。我在这个世界并不违和。我手指上粘着的心松动了。尽管我把它塞到了锡箔和丝巾的下面，却无法彻底挣脱，不过倒也差不多了。

我明白了，坐在那里分析我的心在过去的40年里的每一个动作、每一次悸动、每一次跳动，这是个错误。我的路彻底走错了，走这条路，会让我这颗血淋淋、百味杂陈、大喜过望的心永远地长在我的手上……

哈！你以为我完蛋了！你以为……

看，我一怒之下会把心滚出去，

像个手球似的弹起来，

在墙上，脸上，铁轨上，雨伞上，鸽子的背上……

不行，这么做根本无济于事，只会让情况恶化。我应该做让自己吃惊的事情，就像那个女人、两只鸽子、刺耳的高跟鞋声和真丝般的翅膀让我吃惊一样。

我穿上大衣，把包裹着丝巾的臃肿的手臂端到胸前，这样，若是有人问：你的手怎么了？我就可以答道：手指被门夹了。然后，我走上街头。

在这么多人中间穿行并非易事，我担心他们好奇：那个女人的手怎么了？因为这样一来，我就难以忘我。而我的心一直在我的手上刺痛、抽痛，提醒着我。

我现在出来了，却不知所措。我应该去跟人共进午餐吗？还是去公园逛逛？还是给自己买件衣服？我最后决定独自一人绕着圆湖边转一转。我四天四夜没合眼，想摆脱这颗心。我走到牛津马戏团站搭乘地铁。此时是中午，人山人海。我感觉不自在，当然，却不需要担心。我敢说，在伦敦，你就算全裸走在大街上，都不会有人回头看你一眼。

我上了自动扶梯下月台，看着上行扶梯上从我身旁经过的一张张脸，一如平时。一如平时，我奇怪这些人会与我以这种方式偶遇，我奇怪我们不会再相逢，或者说我们即使再次相逢也不会知道是重逢。一如平时，我走上人头涌动的月台，看着一张张脸。然后，我上了车，车厢里人已经满了，我找到了一个座位。此时车里虽然没有高峰时段那么挤，却也没有空座位了。我累了，于是靠在椅背上，合上眼睛，打定主意要小睡一会儿。我正要睡着的时候，就听到了一个女人的低语抑或宣言：

“一个金烟盒，嗯，是个好东西。对不对，我必须说，一个金烟盒，是的……”

那声音里有某种东西让我睁开了眼睛：在隔间的另一头，跟我隔了八个人的地方，坐着一个身体瘦削、面色苍白的年轻女人，身穿一件廉价的绿色棉布大衣，脚蹬一双棕色平底鞋，腿上穿的是莱尔线长袜，手上没戴手套。她一定很穷——现在，这样打扮的女人已是罕见。她的坐姿让我印象深刻。她半蜷着身体坐着，向左扭过头来，她在直勾勾地看着邻座的一个老男人的肚子。不过，显而易见，她对那个老男人的肚子视而不见，她那双年轻的眼睛显然并没有看任何东西，她看的是内在的东西。

显而易见，她孤身一人，在这拥挤的车厢里，她的行为并没有让别人不自在。我环顾四周，人们性格不同，所以或者在微笑，或者交换着眼色，或者在做鬼脸，或者视而不见，而她却对我们一概视而不见。

突然，她挺起身体，在座位上坐直，凝视着对面的座位，对着对面的座位说道：

“嗯，这么说，你是这么想的，你是这么想的，你是这么想的，对吗？嗯，你以为我当时正在家里等你，而你却给了她一个金盒子，还……”

她那单薄的身体做了一个钟摆动作，顶着一头淡色头发的窄窄的头向左转，眼睛直勾勾地、茫然地盯着那个老男人的肚子，又恢复原来的姿势。老男人不自然地笑了笑。我探身向前，观察跟我坐同一排的人，只见坐在她对面的一个男人，一个年轻的男人，跟那个老男人一样不自在，却决意要保持被逗乐的样子。于是，我们齐刷刷地看着她，这个身体单薄、面色苍白、沉浸在个人不幸里的年轻人。而她却完全没有意识到我们的存在，把心中的所思所想大声地说了出来。还有一次，并没有什么特别的来由和预兆，也不是因为列车在邦德站停靠后再次启动前行把她从睡梦中惊醒，在站与站行进的时候，她向前扭动着身体，对对面座位上的她（那个年轻男人已经下车，现在坐在那里的是一个头发灰白卷曲的美貌的老妇人）说道：

“嗯，我现在知道了，不是吗？如果你满面笑容、欢天喜地地回来，我就会知道的，不是吗？你用不着告诉我，我也知道了，我已经对她说过了，我知道你给了她一个金烟盒……”

说到这里，她又做了一个钟摆动作，她住了口，或者是被打住了话头，或者是说不下去了，她半转身来直勾勾地盯着那个大肚子——那个中年老男人还坐在那里。列车到达大理石拱门站，他下了车，与其说对着整个车厢，不如说对着车厢里的所有人宽容地微微一笑，似乎在说：我敢肯定你们已经意识到，显而易见，明摆着的，这个不幸的女人精神有问题……

他坐过的座位现在空着。大理石拱门站没人上车，那两个站着的男人在等着其他空座，不想坐在她旁边接受她直勾勾的目光。

我们都坐着，目光温柔地看着前面，我们都假装自己不知道，也不知道别人知道那个可怜的女人疯了，所以我们应该出手相助。我甚至不知道该不该对她说：夫人，你疯了——要我送你回家吗？或者说：可怜的人，不要这样啦，没用，你是知道的——离开他算啦，那样他才会清醒过来……

瞧，过了一会儿，控制她的内在机制不再起效时，她转过身来，对那个美貌的老妇人说道，老妇人极力克制着接受了她的指控：

“是，我知道！哦，就是！我的鞋呢？我的鞋呢？她得到了一个金烟盒，这个下流的婊子，一个金盒子……”

停止。扭动。直勾勾地盯着。向着旁边空座。

令人称奇。因为那是一种被冰冻的痛苦，我可怎么形容呢？一种没有激情的激情——我们看到了里面的痛苦，与其说是我们看到了个人悲剧——不如说是人类悲剧的实质。但是，剧中不存在感情。她就像一个正在演出《控夫记》、《薄情郎》或《地下情》的演员，她只管背背台词，只要台词没背错，其他都不顾及。

不论是她半扭着身体的姿势，还是她一眨不眨地盯着青绿色的难堪的毛椅套的眼睛，还是坐直了身体，对对面美貌的老妇人的指控，她那僵硬的样子都很吓人——对，就是她那僵硬的样子吓到了我们。显而易见，她完全可以（如果她内在的机器失灵了的话）保持沉默，永远，或是半扭姿势，或是坐直姿势，或者在半扭半直之间的任何姿势——对，我们都能想象出，她那永远冰冻式的随心所欲的姿势。我们好像看到了某个女人的外壳在做一些规定性的动作。

她根本就不在那里。坐在那里的是什么东西，她是什么人，都无法说清。当然，也不难想象她那瘦削、温柔的小脸粲然一笑，彻底忘却自己此时所扮演的角色。她不知道自己此时正在列车上，列车正行进在大理石拱门站和皇后道之间，她也不知道她在当众指责她的丈夫或者恋人，她也不知道我们在看她。

突然，在丝巾和锡箔下面，我的手指轻了，因为我的心滚落下来了。

我急忙把它从手掌里甩出来，以免再粘上，然后掀开丝巾，把有型有款的完美的心，平放在膝盖上，这颗心像情人节卡上银光闪闪的心，当然，这颗心是三维立体的。与其说这颗心绝对无害，这是用词不当，不如说这颗心小清新，只是正如我刚才说的那样，品位太差。我观察到车厢里的人，现在都不看那个疯女人，转而看着我和我的心，他们很高兴。

我起身，走了大约四步，来到她身旁，把锡箔包裹着的心放到了她直勾勾地盯着的座位上。

开始，她还没反应，接着，她如释重负地呻吟着、低语着，完全是戏剧化的悲哀，她俯身捡起银光闪闪的心，紧紧地抱在怀里，前后摇晃着，甚至把脸偎上去，直勾勾地盯着心尖，仿佛对她的丈夫说：看，我得到了什么，我不再在意你和你的烟盒了，我得到了一颗银光闪闪的心。

车到诺丁山门站，我起身，车厢里的人恭喜我，我在他们赞许的颔首和微笑中下了车。我走出月台，上了上行扶梯，走上大街，进了公园。

没有心了。彻底没有心啦。怎样的极乐。怎样的自由……

听到那个声音了吗？那是笑声，是的。

那是我在笑，是的，那是我。

How I Finally Lost My Heart

It would be easy to say that I picked up a knife, slit open my side, took my heart out, and threw it away; but unfortunately it wasn't as easy as that. Not that I, like everyone else, had not often wanted to do it. No, it happened differently, and not as I expected.

It was just after I had had a lunch and a tea with two different men. My lunch partner I had lived with for (more or less) four and seven-twelfths years. When he left me for new pastures, I spent two years, or was it there, half dead, and my heart was a stone, impossible to carry about, considering all the other things weighting on one. Then I slowly, and with difficulty, got free, because my heart cherished a thousand adhesions to my first love—through from another point of view he could be legitimately described as either my second real love (my father being the first) or my third (my brother intervening).

As the folk song has it:

I have loved but three men in my life,

My father, my brother, and the man that took my life.

But if one were going to look at the thing from outside,

without insight, he could be seen as (perhaps, I forget) the thirteenth, but to do that means disregarding the inner emotional truth. For we all know that those affairs or entanglements one has between serious loves, though they may number dozens and stretch over years, don't really count.

This way of looking at things creates a number of unhappy people, for it is well known that what doesn't really count for me might very well count for you. But there is no way of getting over this difficulty, for a serious love is the most important business in life, or nearly so. At any rate, most of us are engaged in looking for it. Even when we are in fact being very serious indeed with one person we still have an eighth of an eye cocked in case some stranger unexpectedly encountered might turn out to be even more serious. We are all entirely in agreement that we are in the right to taste, test, sip, and sample a thousand people on our way to the real one. It is not too much to say that in our circles tasting and sampling is probably the second most important activity, the first being earning money. Or to put it another way, if you are serious about this thing, you go on laying everybody that offers until something clicks and you're all set to go.

I have digressed from an earlier point; that I regarded this man I had lunch with (we call him A) as my first love; and still do, despite the Freudians, who insist on seeing my father as A and possibly my brother as B, making my (real) first love C. And despite, also, those who might ask: What about your two husbands and all those affairs?

What about them? I did not really love them, the way I loved A.

I had lunch with him. Then, quite by chance, I had tea with B. When I say B, here, I mean my second serious love, not my brother, or the little boys I was in love with between the ages of five and fifteen, if we are going to take fifteen (arbitrarily) as the point of no return...which last phrase is in itself a pretty brave defiance of the secular arbiters.

In between A and B (my count) there were a good many affairs, or samples, but they didn't score. B and I clicked, we went off like a bomb, though not quite as simply as A and I had clicked, because my heart was bruised, sullen, and suspicious because of A's throwing me over. Also there were all those ligaments and adhesions binding me to A still to be loosened, one by one. However, for a time B and I got on like a house on fire, and then we came to grief. My heart was again a ton weight in my side.

If this were a stone in my side, a stone,

I could pluck it out and be free...

Having lunch with A, then tea with B, two men who between them had consumed a decade of my precious years (I am not counting the test or trial affairs in between) and, it is fair to say, had balanced all the delight (plenty and intense) with misery (oh Lord, Lord)—moving from one to the other, in the course of an afternoon, conversing amiably about this and that, with meanwhile my heart going on more than slight reminiscent tugs, the fish of memory as the end of a long slack line…

To sum up, it was salutary.

Particularly as that evening I was expecting to meet C, or someone who might very well turn out to be C, though I don't want to give too much emphasis to C, the truth is I can hardly remember what he looked like, but one can't be expected to remember the unimportant ones one has sipped or tasted in between. But after all, he might have turned out to be C, we might have clicked, and I was in that state of mind (in which we all so often are) of thinking: He might turn out to be the one.(I use a woman's magazine phrase deliberately here, instead of saying, as I might: Perhaps it will be serious.)

So there I was (I want to get the details and atmosphere right) standing at a window looking into a street (Great Portland Street, as a matter of fact) and thinking that while I would not dream of regretting my affairs, or experiences, with A and B (it is better to have loved and lost than never to have loved at all), my anticipant of the heart because of spending an evening with a possible C had a certain unreality, because there was no doubt that both A and B had caused me unbelievable pain. Why, therefore, was I looking forward to C? I should rather be running away as fast as I could.

It suddenly occurred to me that I was looking at the whole

phenomenon quite inaccurately. My (or perhaps I am permitted to say our?) way of looking at it is that one must search for an A, or a B, or a C or a D with a certain combination of desirable or sympathetic qualities so that one may click, or spontaneously combust: or to put it differently, one needs a person who, like a saucer of water, allows one to float off on him or her, like a transfer. But this wasn't so at all. Actually one carries with one a sort of burning spear stuck in one's side, that one waits for someone else to pull out; it is something painful, like a sore or a wound, that one can not wait to share with someone else.

I saw myself quite plainly in a moment of truth: I was standing at a window (on the third floor) with A and B behind me, a rather attractive woman, if I may say so, with a mellowness that I would be the first to admit is the sad harbinger of age, but is attractive by definition, because it is a testament to the amount of sampling and sipping (I nearly wrote "sampling" and "sapping") I have done in my time...There I stood, brushed, dressed, red-lipped, kohl-eyed, all waiting for an evening with a possible C. And at another window overlooking (I think I am right in saying) Margaret Street, stood C, brushed, washed, shaved, smiling: an attractive man (I think) and he was thinking: Perhaps she will turn out to be D (or A or 3 or ? or %, or whatever symbol he used) . We stood, separated by space, certainly, in identical conditions of pleasant uncertainty and anticipation, and we both held our hearts in our hands, all pink and palpitating and ready for pleasure and pain, and we were about to throw these hearts in each other's face like snowballs, or cricket balls (How's that?) or, more accurately, like great bleeding wounds: "Take your wound." Because the last thing one ever thinks at such moments is that he (or she) will say: Take my wound, please remove the spear from my side. No, not at all; one simply expects to get rid of one's own.

I decided I must go to the telephone and say, C!—You know that joke about the joke-makers who don't trouble to tell each other jokes, but simply say Joke 1 or Joke 2, and everyone roars with laughter, or snickers, or giggles appropriately...Actually one could reverse the game by guessing whether it was Joke C (b) or Joke A (d) according to what sort of laughter a person made to match the silent thought...Well, C (I imagined myself saying), the analogy is for or instruction: Let's take the whole thing as real or said. Let's not lick each other's sores; let's keep our hearts to ourselves. Because just consider it, C, how utterly absurd—here we stand at our respective windows with our palpitating hearts in our hands...

At this moment, dear reader, I was forced simply to put down the telephone with an analogy. For I felt the fingers of my left hand push outwards around something rather large, light, and slippery—hard to describe this sensation, really. My hand is not large, and my heart was in a state of inflation after having had lunch with A, tea with B, and then looking forward to C...Anyway, my fingers were stretching out rather desperately to encompass an unknown, largish, lightish object, and I said: Excuse me a minute, to C, looked down, and there was my heart, in my hand.

I had to end the conversation there.

For one thing, to find that one has achieved something so often longed for, so easily, is upsetting. It's not as if I had been trying. To get something one wants simply by accident—no, there's no pleasure in it, no feeling of achievement. So to find myself heart-whole, or, more accurately, heart-less, or at any rate, rid of the damned thing, and at such an awkward moment, in the middle of an imaginary telephone call with a man who might possibly turn out to be C—well, it was irritating rather than not.

For another thing, a heart, raw and bleeding and fresh from one's side, is not the prettiest sight. I'm not going into that at all. I was appalled, and indeed embarrassed that that was what had been loving and beating away all those years, because if I'd had any idea at all—well, enough of that.

My problem was how to get rid of it.

Simple, you'll say, drop it into the waste bucket.

Well, let me tell you, that's what I tried to do. I took a good look at this object, nearly died with embarrassment, and walked over to the rubbish can, where I tried to let it roll off my fingers. It wouldn't. It was stuck. There was my heart, a large red pulsing bleeding repulsive object, stuck to my fingers. What was I going to do? I sat down, lit a cigarette (with one hand, holding the matchbox between my knees) , held my hand with the heart stuck on it over the side of the chair so that it could drip into to a bucket, and considered.

If this were a stone in my hand, a stone,

I could throw it over a tree...

When I had finished the cigarette, I carefully unwrapped some tin foil of the kind used to wrap food in when cooking and I fitted a sort of cover around my heart. This was absolutely and urgently necessary. First, it was smarting badly. After all, it had spent some forty years protected by flesh and ribs, and the air was too much for it. Secondly, I couldn't have any Tom, Dick, and Harry walking in and looking at it. Thirdly, I could not look at it for too long myself, it filled me with shame. The tin foil was effective, and indeed rather striking. It is quite pliable and now it seemed as if there were a stylized heart balanced on my palm, like a globe, in glittering, silvery substance. I almost felt I needed a scepter in the other hand to balance it...But the thing was, there is no other word for it, in bad taste. I then wrapped a scarf around hand and tin-foiled heart, and felt safer. Now it was a question of pretending to have hurt my hand until I could think of a way of getting rid of my heart altogether, short of amputating my hand.

Meanwhile I telephoned (really, not in imagination) C, who

now would never be C. I could feel my heart, which was stuck so close to my fingers that I could feel every beat or tremor, give a gulp of resigned grief at the idea of this beautiful experience now never to be. I told him some idiotic lie about having flu. Well, he was all stiff and indignant, but concealing it urbanely, as I would have done, making a joke but allowing a tiny barb of sarcasm to rankle in the last well-chosen phrase. Then I sat down again to think out my whole situation.

There I sat.

What was I going to do?

There I sat.

I am going to have to skip about four days here, vital enough in all conscience, because I simply can not go heartbeat by heartbeat through my memories. A pity, since I suppose this is what this story is about; but in brief: I drew the curtains, I took the telephone off the hook, I turned on the lights, I took the scarf off the glittering shape, then the tin foil, and then I examined the heart. There were two-fifths of a century's experience to work through, and before I had even got through the first night, I was in a state hard to describe...

Or if I could pull the nerves from my skin,

A quick red net to drag through a sea for fish...

By the end of the fourth day I was worn out. By no act of will, or intention, or desire, could I move that heart by a fraction—

on the contrary, it was not only stuck to my fingers, like a sucked boiled sweet, but was actually growing to the flesh to my fingers and my palm.

I wrapped it up again in tin foil and scarf, and turned out the lights and pulled up the blinds and opened the curtains. It was about ten in the morning, an ordinary London day, neither hot nor cold nor clear nor clouded nor wet nor fine. And while the street is interesting, it is not exactly beautiful, so I wasn't looking at it so much as waiting for something to catch my attention while thinking of something else.

Suddenly I heard a tap-tap-tapping that got louder, sharp and clear, and I knew before I saw her that this was the sound of high heels on a pavement though it might just as well have been a hammer against stone. She walked fast opposite my window and her heels hit the pavement so hard that all the noises of the street seemed absorbed into that single tap-tap-clang-clang. As she reached the corner at Great Portland Street two London pigeons swooped diagonally from the sky very fast, as if they were bullets aimed to kill her; and then as they saw her they swooped up and off at an angle. Meanwhile she had turned the corner. All this has taken time to write down, but the thing happening took a couple of seconds: the woman's body hitting the pavement bang-bang through her heels then sharply turning the corner in a right angle; and the pigeons making anther acute angle across hers and intersecting it in a fast swoop of displaced air. Nothing to all that, of course, nothing—she had gone off down the street, her heels tip-tapping, and the pigeons landed on my windowsill and began cooing. All gone, all vanished, the marvelous exact coordination of sound and movement, but it had happened, it had made me happy and exhilarated, I had no problems in this world, and I realized that the heart stuck to my fingers was quite loose. I couldn't get it off altogether, through I was tugging at it under the scarf and the tin foil, but almost.

I understood that sitting and analyzing each movement or pulse of beat of my heat through forty years was a mistake. I was on the wrong track altogether: this was the way to attach my red, bitter, delighted heart to my flesh for ever and ever...

Ha! So you think I'm done! You think...

Watch, I'll roll my heart in a mesh of rage.

And bounce it like a handball off.

Walls, faces, railings, umbrellas, and pigeons'backs...

No, all that was no good at all, it just made things worse. What I must do is to take myself by surprise, as it were, the way I was taken by surprise over the woman and the pigeons and the sharp sounds of heels and silk wings.

I put on my coat, held my lumpy scarfed arm across my chest, so that if anyone said: What have you done with your hand? I could say: I've banged my finger in the door. Then I walked down into the street.

It wasn't easy to go among so many people, when I was worried that they were thinking: What has that woman down to her hand? Because that made it hard to forget myself. And all the time it tingled and throbbed against my fingers, reminding me.

Now I was out, I didn't know what to do. Should I go and have lunch with someone? Or wander in the park? Or buy myself a dress? I decided to go the Round Pond, and walk around it by myself. I was tired after four days and nights without sleep. I went down into the underground at Oxford Circus, Midday, Crowds of people. I felt self-conscious, but of course need not have worried. I swear you could walk naked down the street in London and no one would ever turn round.

So I went down the escalator and looked at the faces coming up past me on the other side, as I always do; and wondered, as I always do, how strange it is that those people and I should meet by chance in such a way, and how odd that we would never see each other again, or, if we did, we wouldn't know it. And I went onto the crowded platform and looked at the faces as I always do, and got into the train, which was very full, and found a seat. It wasn't as bad as at rush hour, but all the seats were filled. I leaned back and closed my eyes, deciding to sleep a little, being so tired. I was just beginning to doze off when I heard a woman's voice muttering, or rather declaiming:

"A gold cigarette case, well, that's a nice thing, isn't it, I must say, a gold case, yes..."

There was something about this voice which made me open my eyes: on the other side of the compartment, about eight persons away, sat a youngish woman, wearing a cheep green cloth coat, gloveless hands, flat brown shoes, and lisle stockings. She must be rather poor—a woman dressed like this is a rare sight, these days. But it was her posture that struck me. She was sitting half twisted in her seat, so that her head was turned over her left shoulder, and she was looking straight at the stomach of an elderly man next to her. But it was clear she was not seeing it: her young staring eyes were sightless, she was looking inwards.

She was so clearly alone, in the crowded compartment, that it was not as embarrassing as it might have been. I looked around, and people were smiling, or exchanging glances, or winking, or ignoring her, according to their natures, but she was oblivious of us all.

She suddenly aroused herself, turned so that she sat straight in her seat, and directed her voice and her gaze to the opposite seat:

"Well, so that's what you think, you think that, you think that, do you? Well, you think I'm just going to wait at home for you, but you gave her a gold case and..."

And with a clockwork movement of her whole thin person, she turned her narrow pale-haired head sideways over her left shoulder, and resumed her stiff empty stare at the man's stomach. He was grinning uncomfortably. I leaned forward to look along the line of people in the row of seats I sat in, and the man opposite her, a young man, had exactly the same look of discomfort which he was determined to keep amused. So we all looked at her, the young, thin, pale woman in her private drama of misery, who was so completely unconscious of us that she spoke and thought out loud. And again, without particular warming or reason, in between stops, so it wasn't that she was disturbed from her dream by the train stopping at Bond Street, and then jumping forward again, she twisted her body front ways, and addressed the seat opposite her (the young man had got off, and a smart grey-curled matron had got in) :

"Well, I know about it now, don't I? And if you come in all smiling and pleased well then I know, don't I? You don't have to tell me, I know, and I've said to her, I've said, I know he gave you a gold cigarette case..."

At which point, with the same clockwork impulse, she stopped, or was checked, or simply ran out, and turned herself-around to stare at the stomach—the same stomach, for the middle-aged man was still there. But we stopped at Marble Arch and he got out, giving the compartment, rather than the people in it, a tolerant half-smile which said: I am sure I can trust you to realize that this unfortunate woman is stark staring mad...

His seat remained empty. No people got in a Marble Arch, and the two people standing waiting for seats did not want to sit by her to receive her stare.

We all sat, looking gently in front of us, pretending to ourselves and to each other that we didn't know the poor woman was mad and that in fact we ought to be doing something about it. I even wondered what I should say: Madam, you're mad—shall I escort you to your home? Or: Poor thing, don't go on like that, it doesn't do any good, you know—just leave him, that'll bring him to his senses...

And behold, after the interval that was regulated by her inner mechanism had elapsed, she turned back and said to the smart matron who received this statement of accusation with perfect self-command:

"Yes, I know! Oh yes! And what about my shoes? What about them? A golden cigarette case is what she got, the filthy bitch, a golden case..."

Stop. Twist. Stare. At the empty seat by her.

Extraordinary. Because it was a frozen misery, how shall I put it? A passionless passion—we were seeing unhappiness embodied; we were looking at the essence of some private tragedy—rather, Tragedy. There was no emotion in it. She was like an actress doing Accusation, or Betrayed Love, or Infidelity, when she has only just learned her lines and is not bothering to do more than get them right.

And whether she sat in her half-twisted position, her unblinking eyes staring at the greenish, furry, ugly covering of the train seat, or sat straight, directing her accusation to the smart woman opposite, there was a frightening immobility about her—yes, that was why she frightened us. For it was clear that she might very well (if the inner machine ran down) stay silent, forever, in either twisted or straight position, or at any point between them—yes, we could all imagine her, frozen perpetually in some arbitrary pose. It was as if we watched the shell of some woman going through certain predetermined motions.

For she was simply not there. What was there, who she was, it was impossible to fell, though it was easy to imagine her thin, gentle little face breaking into a smile in total forgetfulness of what she was enacting now. She did not know she was in a train between Marble Arch and Queensway, nor that she was publicly accusing her husband of lover, nor that we were looking at her.

Suddenly I felt, under the scarf and the tin foil, a lightening of my fingers, as my heart rolled loose.

I hastily took it off my palm, in case it decided to adhere there again, and I removed the scarf, leaving balanced on my knees a perfect stylized heart, like a silver heart on a Valentine card, though of course it was three-dimensional. This heart was not so much harmless, no that isn't the word, as artistic, but in very bad taste, as

I said. I could see that the people in the train, now looking at me and the heart, and not at the poor madwoman, were pleased with it.

I got up, took the four or so paces to where she was, and laid the tin-foiled heart down on the seat so that it received her stare.

For a moment she did not react, then with a groan or a mutter of relieved and entirely theatrical grief, she leaned forward, picked up the glittering heart, and clutched it in her arms, hugging it and rocking it back and forth, even laying her check against it, while staring over its top at her husband as if to say: Look what I've got, I don't care about you and your cigarette case, I've got a silver heart.

I got up, since we were at Notting Hill Gate, and, followed by the pleased congratulatory nods and smiles of the people left behind, I went out onto the platform, up the escalators, into the street, and along to the park.

No heart. No heart at all. What bliss. What freedom…

Hear that sound? That's laughter, yes.

That's me laughing, yes, that's me.

软性推销

［美国］阿特·布赫瓦尔德

当前经济的问题之一是很难在年轻人中找到好导购。许多刚出大学校门的学生对客户购买动机的兴趣大过卖出一件商品。他们倾向于过分诚实，诚实到对零售业造成严重的破坏。

我的一个朋友在这里，也就是华盛顿开了一家服装店。她给我讲了一个她雇用的一个店员的故事。这个店员是一位年轻的女士，在大学学的是心理学专业。

这就是事情的大致经过：

这位店员（就让我们叫她布兰普顿小姐吧）入职第一天，看到一位女士走进服装店，于是问她是否需要帮忙。

“我想买秋天穿的套装。”那位女士说道。

“要什么价位的呢？”布兰普顿小姐问道。

“无所谓。”那位女士回答。

“那好，让我来问你一个问题：你买这套衣服是因为你需要吗？还是因为你刚刚跟你丈夫打了一架，所以想买件贵重物品来找个平衡呢？”

“你说什么？”

“也许你怀疑他对你有什么背叛行为，你以为这是你报复他的唯一办法吧。”

“我不明白你在说什么。”那位顾客说道。

“人在愤怒的时候去消费，这是代价高昂的敌对行为。我给你的建议是好好考虑几天，设法弥补你们之间的分歧。买一套新套装不会挽救你的婚姻。”

“非常感谢。”那位顾客冷冷地说道，离开了服装店。

“她现在是生我的气了，”布兰普顿小姐对服装店老板说，“不过，不出一星期她就会为我说服她而心存感激。”

我的店主朋友决定让这件事过去算了。可是，当天下午，又有一位顾客进店，布兰普顿小姐问是否需要帮忙。

那位女士说道：“我需要一个让我兴奋的东西。我要去肯尼迪中心，我要穿一件能迷住所有人的衣服。”

布兰普顿小姐说道：“我们有一些漂亮的晚礼服，适合没有安全感的人穿。”

“没有安全感的人？”

“哦，是的，你莫非不知道衣服是女人补偿安全感的重要方式之一吗？”

“我又不是没有安全感的人。”那位女士生气地说道。

“那你又何必要在肯尼迪中心迷住所有人？你为什么不能接受你自己，反而要依赖你穿的衣服？你是一个非常迷人的人，你正在试图掩盖你的内在美。我可以卖给你一件引人注目的新衣服，但是你却永远不会知道人们驻足而目不转睛是为了你还是你穿的衣服。”

这次店老板决定介入了。

“布兰普顿小姐，这位女士既然想要一件晚礼服，就让她看看我们的晚礼服吧。”

“不，”那位顾客说，“你的店员说得对，就为了那么几个赞美，赞美的人其实根本不在意我穿什么，我为什么要花500美元呢？谢谢你对我的帮助，年轻的女士。这些年我一直没有安全感，连我自己都不知道。”

那个顾客走出了服装店。

压断这家服装店老板的最后一根稻草发生在一个小时以后，一位女大学生想买一套热裤套装，布兰普顿小姐给她上了足足30分钟的妇女解放课，接着说道：“你买热裤套装就是为了成为性对象。”

那天夜里，服装店老板在橱窗上竖了一块招牌：招聘店员，心理学专业大学生勿扰。

The Soft Sell

By Art Buchwald

One of the problems with today's economy is that it's very hard to find young people who are good salesmen. Many students coming out of college are more interested in a customer's motivation than they are in closing a sale. They also have a tendency to be too honest, which can play havoc in the retail business.

A friend of mine has a dress shop here in Georgetown, and she told me of the problems she had with a young lady a psychology major, whom she had hired as a salesgirl.

This, in essence, is what happened:

The first day a lady came in the store, and the salesgirl (let us call her Miss Brampton) asked if she could be of help.

"I'd like a suit for the fall," the lady said.

"What price range?" Miss Brampton asked.

"It doesn't make any difference," the lady replied.

"Well, let me ask you this question: Do you want the suit because you need it? Or have you just had a fight with your husband and are trying to get even by making a very expensive purchase?"

"I beg your pardon?" the lady said.

"Perhaps you suspect him of some infidelity, and you think this is the only way you can get back at him."

"I have no idea what you're talking about," the customer said.

"Spending money in anger is a very expensive form of hostility. My advice to you is to think it over for a few days. Try to patch up your differences. Buying a new suit won't save your marriage."

"Thank you very much," he customer said frostily and left the store.

"She's angry with me now," Miss Brampton told the dress shop owner, "but in a week she'll be grateful I talked her out of it."

My friend the shop proprietor decided to let the incident pass; but that afternoon another customer came in, and Miss Brampton asked if she could be of help.

The lady said, "I need something really exciting. I'm going to the Kennedy Center, and I want a dress that will knock everyone dead."

Miss Brampton said, "We have some lovely evening dresses

over here for insecure people."

"Insecure people?"

"Oh, yes. Didn't you know that clothes are one of the main ways women compensate for insecurity?"

"I'm not insecure," the lady said angrily.

"Then why do you want to knock them dead at the Kennedy Center? Why can't you be accepted for yourself instead of what you wear? You are a very attractive person, and you have an inner beauty you try to disguise. I can sell you a new dress that will attract attention, but then you would never know if it were you or the dress that made people stop and stare."

By this time the dress shop owner decided to step in.

"Miss Brampton, if the lady wants an evening dress, let her see our evening dresses."

"No," the customer said. "Your girl is right. Why spend five hundred dollars to get a few compliments from people who really don't care what I wear? Thank you for helping me, young lady. It's true I've been insecure all these years and didn't even know it."

The customer walked out of the store.

The final straw for the dress store owner took place an hour later when a coed came in to buy a hotpants outfit, and Miss Brampton gave her thirty minutes on women's lib and then said, "All you do when you buy hotpants is to become a sex object."

That night the dress shop owner put a sign in the window: help wanted—no psychology majors need apply.

我的名字叫杂种狗

［美国］凯姆·哈默斯

“你为什么大白天赤身裸体地睡在公园的长凳子上？”

“哦，警官你看，是这么回事，这一切都与早上发生的事情有关，当时我刚醒……”

“大主人的闹钟一响我便从我的狗床上一跃而起，信步进了厨房，因为我知道大主人肯定要到这里来。我坐在猫小姐旁边，等待着我们的早餐。（对，我们猫狗同在一个屋檐下，还相处得非常好呢。）”

“住嘴，什么狗床不狗床的？”

“嗨，其实我就是一条狗。不管怎样，你让我解释完。不论怎样，大主人一下楼，看他匆匆忙忙跑来跑去的样子，我们就能够感觉到今天会是忙碌的一天。我们猜也许闹钟响迟了。

“主人匆匆给我们喂了食以后就冲出了房门，自己都没顾上吃早餐。不过这相当正常，大主人早上总是来不及吃早餐。

“我们吃完早餐，猫小姐走到窗前，坐在窗台上晒太阳。与此同时，我上了楼。我知道此时小主人和小公主该起床了，大主人忘记叫醒他们了。我走进小主人的房间先把他弄醒，然后穿过走廊来到小公主的房间里，我跳到了床上舔她的脸蛋，把她也弄醒了。

“最后我必须叫醒大夫人。我最后一个叫醒她是因为我知道她最恨早起，所以我小心翼翼地走进大夫人的房间，来到她的床边，轻轻地推她身体的一侧。不幸的是，我的鼻子刚挨到她身体的一侧，她就直直地跳了起来对我大喊大叫，要我滚出房间，我立刻滚了出去。

“我闲逛到走廊，又下了楼。小主人和小公主已经在楼下吃起了早饭，尽管他们快迟到了，可是他们仍然穿着睡衣。我知道我应该想方设法催促他们加快速度，于是我请猫小姐帮忙。

“猫小姐赞同我的计划。于是，我假装撵她，她一下子就跳到了餐桌上，‘不小心’打翻了它们的谷类食品，溅到了到他们的膝盖上。两个小家伙跳了起来，赶紧跑到楼上去换衣服，哈哈，我的计划大功告成啦！

“夫人这个时候下了楼。她手脚麻利地收拾好弄得一团糟的早餐，接着就开始为两个孩子准备中餐。她把中餐放进门旁的书包里，然后大声喊说他们该走了，否则就要迟到了。

“两个孩子都冲下楼来，抓起他们的书包就出了门。我像平常那样，从我的狗门里出来，像每天早晨都做的那样跟在他们身后，确保他们一路平安到学校。

“当我从学校回家的时候，有辆厢式货车停在我的身边。紧接着我发现自己被一张网罩住了，然后被扔到后面的车厢里。我在车厢里拼命挣扎、叫喊，期望有人来救我，什么人都行。可是一点儿用也没有，旁边那个劫持我的家伙看我这么挣扎，就给我打了一针让我安静下来。

“我记得的接下来的事是，当我醒过来的时候，发现自己躺在一张床上。我坐起来，东张西望，想弄明白我在哪里。我意识到了原来我在一间科学实验室里，被拴在床上。我低头看看自己，很吃惊地发现自己跟原来不一样了：我不再是一条狗，我成了一个人！

“我吓坏了，开始大喊救命。一个男人走了进来，看了看我，然后对另一个人大声喊起来。另外一个男人也冲了进来，看了看我就转身和刚才那个人几乎同时欢呼了起来：‘成功啦！成功啦！’

“他们中间有一个人走到我的身边，又给我打了一针镇静剂。

“接下来发生的事情是你来到了我的身边，用警棍戳我，把我吓醒了。这就是我怎么会大白天赤身裸体地躺在公园长凳子上的全过程。”

“你说的听起来很有趣，那么孩子，你现在跟我走。顺便问一句，你叫什么名字？”

“我的名字叫杂种狗！”

The Dog

By Kym Hams

"What are you doing asleep on a park bench in the middle of the day naked?"

"Well, you see officer; it all started this morning, when I woke up..."

"I woke up to the sound of big masters' alarm clock and jumped off my doggy bed. I wandered down into the kitchen where I knew big master was headed and sat down next to miss kitty to wait for breakfast. (Yes, we have a cat and a dog in the same house. Surprisingly we get on very well.)"

"Hang on! What do you mean doggy bed?"

"Well, I am actually a dog. Let me finish my explanation. Anyways, when big master came downstairs we could tell that this was going to be a busy day, by the way he was rushing around. We guessed that the alarm clock had gone off late and we were right.

"He fed us quickly and ran out the door, not even bothering to get some breakfast for himself. This was fairly normal, big master hardly ever ate in the mornings.

"We finished our breakfast soon afterward, and Miss Kitty went and sat on the windowsill in the sun. Meanwhile, I went upstairs. I knew little master and little mistress had to get up now, and big master had forgotten to wake them. I walked into little masters' room first and woke him up. Next I went across the hallway and into little mistresses' room. I jumped onto her bed and licked her face, waking her up.

"The last person I had to wake up was big mistress. I left her till last because I knew how much she hates getting woken up. So I cautiously walked into the big room and went to big mistresses' side of the bed. I nudged at her side, trying to wake her up gently. Unfortunately as soon as my nose touched her side, she jumped straight up and yelled at me to get out of her room. I did that straight away.

"I wandered back down the hallway and headed downstairs again. The little master and mistress were already downstairs eating breakfast, but they were still in their pajamas and they were running late. I knew I had to hurry them along somehow so I went and asked Miss Kitty for help.

"She agreed to my plan, so I pretended to chase her and she jumped up on the breakfast counter and 'accidentally' split their cereal into their laps. Both of them immediately jumped up and ran upstairs to change. My plan worked!

"Big mistress came downstairs just then. She quickly cleaned up the mess left from breakfast and started making little master and mistress lunches. She put these in their bags which were near the door and yelled out that they had to leave now or they were going to be late.

"Both of them ran downstairs and grabbed their bags on the way out the door. I followed them out the doggy door as usual and made sure they got to school safely, just like I did every morning.

"As I was walking home, I saw a van pull up beside me and next thing I know I'm stuck in a net and being tossed into the back of the van. I started struggling and barking, hoping someone, anyone, would come rescue me. It didn't help, as my abductor noticed my struggle and decided to give me a tranquilizing needle to calm me down.

"The next thing I remembered was when I woke up, I was lying on a bed. I sat up and looked around, trying to work out where I was. I realized I was in a science lab and I was chained to the bed. I looked down at myself, and that's when I realized something was different. I wasn't a dog anymore! I was human!

"I freaked then. I started yelling for help and a man walked in. He looked at me and yelled out to someone else. Another man raced in, looked at me then he turned to the first man and they both started shouting, 'It worked! It worked!'

"One of them walked over to me then and stabbed me with

another tranquilizing needle.

"Next thing I remember you came along and started poking me with your baton officer and you scared me awake. So that's my story as to how I ended up asleep on a park bench in the middle of the day naked."

"Very funny son, now you're coming with me. Buy the way, what's your name?"

"My name's Mutt..."

世界末日的前夜

［美国］雷·布莱伯利

“如果你知道这是世界的最后一个晚上，你会做什么？”

“我会做什么，你的意思是，真的？”

“是的，真的。”

“我不知道——我没想过。”她把银质咖啡壶的把手转到他那边，把两个杯子放到茶碟上。

他倒了点儿咖啡。在后院，两个小女孩在绿色飓风灯的照射下在客厅地毯上玩积木。傍晚的空气中有一股清爽的煮好的咖啡香气。

“好吧，最好开始考虑一下。”他说。

“你不是故意的吧？”他的妻子说。

他点点头。

“战争？”

他摇了摇头。

“不是氢弹或者原子弹？”

“不是。”

“还是细菌战？”

“根本不是这些。”他一边说，一边慢慢搅动着咖啡，凝视着咖啡的黑色深处。“但就在一本书的结尾，让我们假设一下。”

“我还是不明白。”

“是的，我也没真正弄明白。这只是一种感觉，有时它让我害怕，有时我一点儿也不害怕——而是平静的。”他瞥了一眼姑娘们，她们的黄头发在明亮的灯光下流光溢彩，然后他压低了声音。“我没告诉你，四天前我经历过一次。”

“什么？”

“我做了一个梦。我梦见一切都会结束，一个声音说是的。我什么声音都不记得了，但无论如何就是那个声音，它说地球上的一切都会停止。第二天早上醒来的时候，我没想太多，可是后来我去上班，这种感觉好像一整天都萦绕在我的脑海。那天下午，我看到斯坦威利斯从窗户往外看，我说：‘告诉我，你在想什么。’他说：‘我昨晚做了一个梦，’在他告诉我这个梦之前，我就知道是什么梦了。我本可以告诉他，但他告诉了我，我听了他说的话。”

“是同一个梦吗？”

“是的。我告诉斯坦我也梦到了。他似乎并不惊讶。事实上，他如释重负。然后我们开始穿过办公室，该死的。这不是事先计划好的。我们没说话，就在附近走走吧。我们自顾自地走着，到处都能看到人们看着自己的桌子、自己的手或窗外，却不看眼前的东西。我和他们中的几个人说话，斯坦也跟我一样。”

“他们都做梦了？”

“都做了。同一个梦，没有区别。”

“你相信梦吗？”

“是的。我从未这么确定过。”

“什么时候到？世界末日，我是说。”

“在我们的某个夜晚，随着夜幕降临，世界各地的人，那些前进的部分也将消失。要花 24 个小时才能全部结束。”

他们坐了一会儿，没有碰咖啡。然后他们慢慢地把它端起来喝了，同时看着对方。

“我们活该如此吗？”她问道。

“这不是应该不应该的问题，只是事情没有解决。我注意到你甚至没有为此争辩过。为什么不呢？”

“我想我是有一个理由的。”她说。

“跟办公室里每个人都一样的理由吗？”

她点了点头。“我什么都不想说。这事发生在昨天，街区里的女人都在谈论此事，在她们中间。”她拿起晚报给他看。“新闻对此只字未提。”

“不，人尽皆知，还有什么必要提？”他接过报纸，往椅背上一靠，先看了姑娘们一眼，然后又看了她一眼。“你怕了吗？”

“不怕，我甚至都不为孩子们害怕。我以前一直以为我会怕死，可是现在死到临头了，我却不怕。”

“科学家们一直喋喋不休的自卫本能精神哪里去了？”

“我不知道。但你觉得事物合乎逻辑的时候，就不会太激动。这件事合乎逻辑。从我们的生活方式只能生发出这样的结果。”

“我们过得还不太差，是吧？”

“不差，经济上不差。我推测这正是麻烦所在。我们除了自己之外什么都不是，与此同时，世界上大部分地区都在忙着做非常可怕的事情。”

姑娘们在客厅里笑着挥手，从她们街区的房子里摔了下来。

“我一直想象人们在现在这种时候会在大街上尖叫。”

“我猜不会，人不会对真实的事情尖叫。”

“你知道吗？除了你和女儿，我不会想念任何人。除了你们三个，我从来都没有喜欢过城市、汽车、工厂、我的工作。除了我的家人，可能还有天气变化，天气热的时候一杯清凉的水，舒舒服服地睡一觉，我什么都不会想念。都是小事，真的。我们怎么能坐在这里这么说话？”

“因为再没有别的事情可做。”

“是这样，当然，如果我们有事可做，我们就会做的。我猜这是有史以来，第一次人人都确切地知道自己在这个世界上的最后一夜在做什么。”

“我想知道别人现在、今晚、在接下来的几个小时里做什么？”

“像平时那样，去看演出，听收音机，看电视，打扑克，给孩子收拾上床睡觉，自己上床睡觉。”

“用某种值得自豪的方式——像平时那样。”

“我们都不差。”

他们坐了一会儿，然后都倒了点儿咖啡喝。“你为什么猜是今晚呢？”

“因为。”

“为什么不是曾经的19世纪的最后十年，或者是五个世纪以前、十个世纪以前呢？”

“可能因为历史上还从来没有过1951年2月30日，现在正是，那就是它了，因为这个日期比其他日期更重要，还因为全世界情况都一样，所以就是世界末日。”

“今夜海洋双向航线上有轰炸机，它们再也见不到陆地了。”

“这也是部分原因。”

“好了，”他说道，“接下来干什么？洗碟子？”

他们仔细地洗了碟子，特别地把它们整整齐齐地摞起来。八点半的时候，他们把姑娘们收拾上床，亲吻她们，道了晚安，打开了她们床边的小灯，门开了一条缝。

“我想知道。”丈夫说，走出去回头看了看，手里拿着烟斗在那里站了一会儿。

“什么？”

“门应该一直关着，还是应该让它半开一点儿，这样我们就能听到她们的呼唤。”

“我想知道孩子们是否知道——有人向他们提起过吗？”

“没有，当然没有。有的话她们会问我们的。”

他们坐着看报纸，聊着天，听着收音机里的音乐，然后一起坐在壁炉旁，看着炭火的余烬，这时钟敲了十点半、11 点和 11 点半。他们想到了世界上所有其他度过了他们最后夜晚的人，每个人都有自己独特的方式。

“好吧。”他终于说道。他吻了妻子很长时间。

“不管怎样，我们彼此都很好。”

“你想哭吗？”他问。

“不想。”

他们穿过房子，关上所有的灯，锁上所有的房门，走进卧室，站在凉爽的黑暗中脱去衣服。她把床单从床上拿下来，像往常一样小心地叠在椅子上，然后推开被子。“床单又凉又干净又漂亮。”她说道。

“我累了。”

“我们都累了。”

他们上床躺下。

“等一下。”她说。

他听见她站起来，走到屋后，然后他听到一扇摆动的门轻轻地摇晃着。一会儿她回来了。“厨房里的水一直在流。”她说。“我把水龙头关了。”

这件事这么好笑，他忍不住哈哈大笑。

她和他一起哈哈大笑，知道自己做了什么，真是太好笑了。他们终于停止了大笑，躺在凉爽的深夜的床铺上，他们手拉着手，头挨着头。

“晚安。”过了一会儿，他说道。

“晚安，”她轻声说道，“亲爱的……”

The Last Night of the World

By Ray Bradbury

"What would you do if you knew this was the last night of the world?"

"What would I do? You mean, seriously?"

"Yes, seriously."

"I don't know—I hadn't thought. " She turned the handle of the silver coffeepot toward him and placed the two cups in their saucers.

He poured some coffee. In the background, the two small girls were playing blocks on the parlor rug in the light of the green hurricane lamps. There was an easy, clean aroma of brewed coffee in the evening air.

"Well, better start thinking about it," he said.

"You don't mean it?" said his wife.

He nodded.

"A war?"

He shook his head.

"Not the hydrogen or atom bomb?"

"No."

"Or germ warfare?"

"None of those at all," he said, stirring his coffee slowly and staring into its black depths. "But just the closing of a book, let's say."

"I don't think I understand."

"No, nor do I really. It's just a feeling; sometimes it frightens me, sometimes I'm not frightened at all—but peaceful." He glanced in at the girls and their yellow hair shining in the bright lamplight, and lowered his voice. "I didn't say anything to you. It first happened about four nights ago."

"What?"

"A dream I had. I dreamt that it was all going to be over and a voice said it was; not any kind of voice I can remember, but a voice anyway, and it said things would stop here on Earth. I didn't think too much about it when I awoke the next morning, but then I went to work and the feeling as with me all day. I caught Stan Willis looking out the window in the middle of the afternoon and I said, 'Penny for your thoughts, Stan,' and he said, 'I had a dream last night,' and before he even told me the dream, I knew what it was. I could have told him, but he told me and I listened to him."

"It was the same dream?"

"Yes. I told Stan I had dreamed it, too. He didn't seem surprised. He relaxed, in fact. Then we started walking through offices, for the hell of it. It wasn't planned. We didn't say, let's walk around. We just walked on our own, and everywhere we saw people looking at their desks or their hands or out the windows and not seeing what was in front of their eyes. I talked to a few of them; so did Stan."

"And all of them had dreamed?"

"All of them. The same dream, with no difference."

"Do you believe in the dream?"

"Yes. I've never been more certain."

"And when will it stop? The world, I mean."

"Sometime during the night for us, and then, as the night goes on around the world, those advancing portions will go, too. It'll take twenty-four hours for it all to go."

They sat awhile not touching their coffee. Then they lifted it slowly and drank, looking at each other.

"Do we deserve this?" she said.

"It's not a matter of deserving, it's just that things didn't work out. I notice you didn't even argue about this. Why not?"

"I guess I have a reason," she said.

"The same reason everyone at the office had?"

She nodded. "I didn't want to say anything. It happened last night. And the women on the block are talking about it, just among themselves." She picked up the evening paper and held it toward him. "There's nothing in the news about it."

"No, everyone knows, so what's the need?" He took the paper and sat back in his chair, looking at the girls and then at her. "Are you afraid?"

"No. Not even for the children. I always thought I would be frightened to death, but I'm not."

"Where's that spirit of self-preservation the scientists talk about so much?"

"I don't know. You don't get too excited when you feel things are logical. This is logical. Nothing else but this could have happened from the way we've lived."

"We haven't been too bad, have we?"

"No, nor enormously good. I suppose that's the trouble. We haven't been very much of anything except us, while a big part of the world was busy being lots of quite awful things."

The girls were laughing in the parlor as they waved their hands and tumbled down their house of blocks.

"I always imagined people would be screaming in the streets at a time like this."

"I guess not. You don't scream about the real thing."

"Do you know, I won't miss anything but you and the girls. I never liked cities or autos or factories or my work or anything except you three. I won't miss a thing except my family and perhaps the change in the weather and a glass of cool water when the weather's hot, or the luxury of sleeping. Just little things, really. How can we sit here and talk this way?"

"Because there's nothing else to do."

"That's it, of course, for if there were, we'd be doing it. I suppose this is the first time in the history of the world that everyone has really known just what they were going to be doing during the last night."

"I wonder what everyone else will do now, this evening, for the next few hours."

"Go to a show, listen to the radio, watch the TV, play cards, put the children to bed, get to bed themselves, like always."

"In a way that's something to be proud of—like always."

"We're not all bad."

They sat a moment and then he poured more coffee. "Why do you suppose it's tonight?"

"Because."

"Why not some night in the past ten years of in the last century, or five centuries ago or ten?"

"Maybe it's because it was never February 30, 1951, ever before in history, and now it is and that's it, because this date means more than any other date ever meant and because it's the year when things are as they are all over the world and that's why it's the end."

"There are bombers on their course both ways across the ocean tonight that'll never see land again."

"That's part of the reason why."

"Well," he said. "What shall it be? Wash the dishes?"

They washed the dishes carefully and stacked them away with especial neatness. At eight-thirty the girls were put to bed and kissed good night and the little lights by their beds turned on and the door left a trifle open.

"I wonder," said the husband, coming out and looking back, standing there with his pipe for a moment.

"What?"

"If the door should be shut all the way or if it should be left just a little ajar so we can hear them if they call."

"I wonder if the children know—if anyone mentioned anything to them?"

"No, of course not. They'd have asked us about it."

They sat and read the papers and talked and listened to some radio music and then sat together by the fireplace looking at the charcoal embers as the clock struck ten-thirty and eleven and eleven-thirty. They thought of all the other people in the world who had spent their evening, each in their own special way.

"Well," he said at last. He kissed his wife for a long time.

"We've been good for each other, anyway."

"Do you want to cry?" he asked.

"I don't think so."

They went through the house and turned out the lights and locked the doors, and went into the bedroom and stood in the night cool darkness undressing. She took the spread from the bed and folded it carefully over a chair, as always, and pushed back the covers. "The sheets are so cool and clean and nice," she said.

"I'm tired."

"We're both tired."

They got into bed and lay back.

"Wait a moment," she said.

He heard her get up and go out into the back of the house, and then he heard the soft shuffling of a swinging door. A moment later she was back. "I left the water running in the kitchen," she said. "I turned the faucet off."

Something about this was so funny that he had to laugh.

She laughed with him, knowing what it was that she had done that was so funny. They stopped laughing at last and lay in their cool night bed, their hands clasped, their heads together.

"Good night," he said, after a moment.

"Good night," she said, adding softly, "dear..."

烤猪论文

[英国]查尔斯·兰姆

我的朋友曼宁曾热心地给我朗读并讲解过一部中国书的手抄本。上面说，人类在最初的七万年里茹毛饮血，从活的野兽身上生吞活剥，大嚼大吃，跟今天的阿比西尼亚人的做派毫无二致。他们的大圣人孔夫子在他那部《春秋》第二章里非常明确地提到一个人类的黄金时代，被称为“厨芳”，字面意思就是“厨师的芳辰”。这部手抄本接着写道，烤肉，或者不如说烧肉（我认为它是猪肉烹饪中的老大）的技术，是人在无意之中发现的。情况是这样的：

一天清早，养猪人何悌像往常那样，去树林里给猪采集橡果，就把小屋交给他那个笨笨傻傻的大儿子宝宝照看。那么大的孩子一般都爱玩火，宝宝也不例外。谁料宝宝玩起火来火花四溅，溅到一捆干草上，干草见火就着，火势蔓延，他们那间可怜的庭院就全都被点着了，最后化为一片灰烬。被烧的除了茅草屋（那只是没发大水以前草草搭建起来的一间极其简陋的小屋，你可以想象的），更重要的是，刚刚生下的一窝膘肥体壮的小猪，至少有九头，也都被烧死了。

根据我们读过的远古时期的记载，中国猪在整个东方一直被奉为食品里的珍品。当时的宝宝吓得惊慌失措，主要不是因为房子被烧掉了，因为那种房子他父亲和他只要拿上几根干树枝，花上一两个钟头，就能轻而易举地再盖起来。他惊慌失措是因为小猪被烧死了。面对着一具还冒着烟的意外丧生的小猪尸体，他搓着手，一筹莫展，就在这时，一股以前从来没有闻到过的气味飘进了他的鼻孔。这味道是从哪儿来的呀？——自然不是被烧的房子的味道——那种味道他以前又不是没闻到过——因为这个爱玩火的倒霉孩子绝对不是第一次由于粗心大意闯下这种祸。而且，这更不像他所熟悉的香草、杂草或鲜花的味道。同时，好像有了一种预感似的，口水顺着他那下嘴唇一个劲儿地往下流。他怎么想也想不明白。接下来，他弯下身子，摸了摸那头小猪，看看还有没有一点儿生命体征。结果他的手指被烫了，他赶快把手指头缩了回来，放到嘴边，傻傻地吹着。几片烧焦的猪皮碎片碰巧粘在他的手指上，就这样，生平第一次（的确，这也是人类第一次，因为在他以前谁也没有尝到过）——他尝到了——脆脆的猪皮的味道！他又摸了摸小猪，此时小猪的身体已经不那么烫手了，可是他还是有点儿条件反射似的又舔了舔手指。他那迟钝的大脑这才慢慢回过味儿来：原来，扑鼻的香味来自这头被烧焦了的小猪，被烧过的小猪吃起来味道还那么香。他完全沉醉在自己这个新发现的快乐里了，把烧熟了的小猪连皮带肉一大把一大把地扯下来，像野兽似的狼吞虎咽地往嘴里塞——这时候，他的父亲手里拿着打人的棍棒，从还在冒烟的檩椽中间走进来了，一看家里的惨状，手里的棍棒像下冰雹似的密集地打在这个年轻人的肩膀上，可是宝宝就像被苍蝇叮了几口似的，理也不理。他肚子所感受到的快乐让他对于距离肚子那么远的部位的疼痛几乎麻木了。不管他父亲怎么打，也无法让他舍弃那头小猪。直到他把那头小猪全吃下肚，他才意识到自己的处境。就这样，父子之间有了如下对话。

“你个没羞没臊的小崽子，你刚才狼吞虎咽地在吃什么？就因为你搞的恶作剧，房子都烧了三次了，你还嫌不够吗？你个该死的，你刚才一定是在吃火，吃——我也不知道你在吃什么，我问你，你往嘴里塞的是什么东西啊？”

“哦，爸爸，小猪，小猪！你一定要过来尝尝烧过的猪有多香。”

何悌听了，吓得耳朵里嗡的一声。他骂他的儿子，也骂自己生了这么一个儿子，竟然吃烧过的猪。

宝宝的嗅觉在这个早晨变得异常敏锐。他迅速又找出一头小猪，一撕两半儿，把小半个硬塞进何悌的手里，大声说：“吃，吃，吃烧猪吧，爸爸，你尝一口——哦，老天爷！”——他一边这么粗野地喊叫着，一边把那一半往自己嘴里塞，吃得好像都噎住了。

何悌把这该死的玩意儿抓在手里，浑身关节都在打战，他心里犹豫着，究竟要不要把儿子当作一个妖怪处死；这时，烧得脆脆的猪皮把他的手指烫了一下，就像他的儿子一样，而他也把手指放到了嘴边吹了吹，结果尝到了烧猪的滋味。此时的他虽然嘴上还硬说不好吃，其实心里清楚那味道确实很香。最后（手抄本此处的描述有点儿冗长乏味），父子二人索性坐下来大快朵颐，把剩下的那窝小猪很快吃了个精光。

何悌对着宝宝千叮咛万嘱咐，严禁他泄露秘密，否则街坊邻居肯定要把他们当作一对邪恶坏人用石头砸死，因为他们竟敢改变上帝赐给他们的美食。尽管这样，千奇百怪的流言还是传开了。有人发现，何悌家的茅屋被火烧的频率比往常更高。从那时起，他们家火灾不断：有时大白天突然起火，有时深夜里起火。常常是母猪一下崽，何悌家的房子就一定会着火。更引人注意的是何悌的做法，他非但没有为此责罚他的儿子，反而对他更加纵容。后来，他们受到了严密的监视，那个可怕的秘密终于被发现了，于是，父子二人都被传唤到了北京，那时的北京还只是一个无足轻重的小城市。需要提供证据，所以那种令人“憎恶”的食物也被送上了法庭，但在判决之前，陪审团团长请求将烧猪肉拿到陪审席上审查。然后，他摸了摸，陪审员们也都摸了摸，他们的手指都被烫了，就像宝宝和他父亲曾经被烫过一样，不仅如此，他们很自然地一个个也都把手指伸到了嘴边去吹；结果，在所有的证据面前，在法官明明白白的指控面前——让法庭上所有的人，包括市民、外乡人、记者和一切旁听者全都大吃一惊的是——陪审团既没有离开席位，也没有商议，就一致做出了“无罪”的裁决。

那位法官是个狡猾的家伙，对于这种明显不合法律程序的决定装聋作哑。刚一退庭，他就鬼鬼祟祟地把那些小猪全都据为己有。还没过几天，有人发现法官老爷的公馆就着了火。不仅如此，这种事就像长了翅膀，四面八方都能看到火光冲天。这一地区的柴火和生猪价格飞涨，保险公司纷纷关门大吉。一天一天过去，人们盖的房子愈来愈简陋，到后来简直让人担心：建筑这门学问恐怕不久就要在人间失传。就这样，点房子烧猪的习惯就流传下来了。那个手抄本写道，随着时间的推移，某位类似我国的洛克那样的大贤人诞生了，这才发现，猪肉也好，别的什么动物的肉也好，要想烹制为食品（或者，用他们的说法叫烧熟），根本不需要把整幢房子都烧掉。于是，原始的烤肉架出现了。把肉串起来或用铁叉烤肉的办法在一两个世纪以后也出现了，不过在哪朝哪代我可记不清。那部手抄本在结束时写道，人类的那些最有用、最是一目了然的技艺，就是这样一步一步慢慢地发展起来的。

A Dissertation Upon Roast Pig

By Charles Lamb

Mankind, says a Chinese manuscript, which my friend M. was obliging enough to read and explain to me, for the first seventy thousand ages ate their meat raw, clawing or biting it from the living animal, just as they do in Abyssinia to this day. This period is not obscurely hinted at by their great Confucius in the second chapter of his Mundane Mutations, where he designates a kind of golden age by the term Cho-fang, literally the Cook's holiday. The manuscript goes on to say, that the art of roasting or rather broiling (which I take to be the elder brother) was accidentally discovered in the manner following.

The swineherd, Ho-ti, having gone out into the woods one morning, as his manner was, to collect mast for his hogs, left his cottage in the care of his eldest son Bo-bo, a great lubberly boy, who being fond of playing with fire, as youngsters of his age commonly are, let some sparks escape into a bundle of straw, which kindling quickly, spread the conflagration over every part of their poor mansion, till it was reduced to ashes. Together with the cottage (a sorry antediluvian makeshift of a building, you may think it), what was of much more importance, a fine litter of new-farrowed pigs, no less than nine in number, perished.

China pigs have been esteemed a luxury all over the East from the remotest periods that we read of. Bo-bo was in the utmost consternation, as you may think, not so much for the sake of the tenement, which his father and he could easily build up again with a few dry branches, and the labour of an hour or two, at any time, as for the loss of the pigs. While he was thinking what he should say to his father, and wringing his hands over the smoking remnants of one of those untimely sufferers, an odor assailed his nostrils, unlike any scent which he had before experienced. What could it proceed from?—not from the burnt cottage—he had smelt that smell before—indeed this was by no means the first accident of the kind which had occurred through the negligence of this unlucky young firebrand. Much less did it resemble that of any known herb, weed, or flower. A premonitory moistening at the same time overflowed his nether lip. He knew not what to think. He next stooped down to feel the pig, if there were any signs of life in it. He burned his fingers, and to cool them he applied them in his booby fashion to his mouth. Some of the crumbs of the scorched skin had come away from his fingers, and for the first time in his life (in the world's life indeed, for before him no man had known it) he tasted—crackling! Again he felt and fumbled at the pig. It did not burn him so much now, still he licked his fingers from a sort of habit. The truth at length broke into his slow understanding, that it was the pig that smelt so, and the pig that tasted so delicious; and surrendering himself up to the new-born pleasure, he fell to tearing up whole handfuls of the scorched skin with the flesh next it, and was cramming it down his throat in his beastly fashion, when his sire entered amid the smoking rafters, armed with retributory cudgel, and finding how affairs stood, began to rain blows upon the young rogue's shoulders, as thick as hailstones, which Bo-bo heeded not any more than if they had been flies. The tickling pleasure, which he experienced in his lower regions, had rendered him quite callous to any inconveniences he might feel in those remote quarters. His father might lay on, but he could not beat him from his pig, till he had fairly made an end of it, when, becoming a little more sensible of his situation, something like the following dialogue ensued.

"You graceless whelp, what have you got there devouring? Is it not enough that you have burned me down three houses with your dog's tricks, and be hanged to you! but you must be eating fire, and I know not what—what have you got there, I say?"

"Oh, Father, the pig, the pig! Do come and taste how nice the burnt pig eats."

The ears of Ho-ti tingled with horror. He cursed his son, and he cursed himself that ever he should beget a son that should eat burnt pig.

Bo-bo, whose scent was wonderfully sharpened since morning, soon raked out another pig, and fairly rending it asunder, thrust the lesser half by main force into the fists of Ho-ti, still shouting out "Eat, eat, eat the burnt pig, Father, only taste—Oh Lord!" —with suchlike barbarous ejaculations, cramming all the while as if he would choke.

Ho-ti trembled in every joint while he grasped the abominable thing, wavering whether he should not put his son to death for an unnatural young monster, when the crackling scorching his fingers, as it had done his son's, and applying the same remedy to them, he in his turn tasted some of its flavour, which, make what sour mouths he would for a pretence, proved not altogether displeasing to him. In conclusion (for the manuscript here is a little tedious) both the father and his son fairly sat down to the mess, and never left off till they had dispatched all that remained of the litter.

Bo-bo was strictly enjoined not to let the secret escape, for the neighbors would certainly have stoned them for a couple of abominable wretches, who could think of improving upon the good meat which God had sent them. Nevertheless, strange stories got about. It was observed that Ho-ti's cottage was burned down now more frequently than ever. Nothing but fires from this time forward. Some would break out in broad day, others in the night-time. As often as the sow farrowed, so sure was the house of Ho-ti to be in a blaze; and Ho-ti himself, which was the more remarkable, instead of chastising his son, seemed to grow more indulgent to him than ever. At length they were closely watched, the terrible mystery discovered, and the father and his son summoned to take their trial at Peking, then an inconsiderable assize town. Evidence was given, the obnoxious food itself produced in court, and verdict about to be pronounced, when the foreman of the jury begged that some of the burnt pig, of which the culprits stood accused, might be handed into the box. He handled it, and they all handled it, and burning their fingers, as Bo-bo and his father had done before them, and nature prompting to each of them the same remedy, against the face of all the facts, and the clearest charge which judge had ever given—to the surprise of the whole court, townsfolk, strangers, reporters, and all present—without leaving the box, or any manner of consultation whatever, they brought in a simultaneous verdict of Not Guilty.

The judge, who was a shrewd fellow, winked at the manifest iniquity of the decision; and, when the court was dismissed, went privily, and bought up all the pigs that could be had for love or money. In a few days his Lordship's townhouse was observed to be on fire. The thing took wing, and now there was nothing to be seen but fires in every direction. Fuel and pigs grew enormously dear all over the district. The insurance offices one and all shut up shop. People built slighter and slighter every day, until it was feared that the very science of architecture would in no long time be lost to the world. Thus this custom of firing houses continued, till in process of time, says my manuscript, a sage arose, like our Locke, who made a discovery, that the flesh of swine, or indeed of any other animal, might be cooked (burned, as they called it) without the necessity of consuming a whole house to dress it. Then first began the rude form of a gridiron. Roasting by the string, or spit came in a century or two later, I forget in whose dynasty. By such slow degrees, concludes the manuscript, do the most useful and seemingly the most obvious arts, make their way among mankind.

书写自己的结局

“不管你信不信，我确实有。”

古德温·布朗活在未来。不幸的是，他的父母并不是这样。

“你有这种想象力，将来有一天说不定可以去好莱坞。”他父亲说道。

古德温的父亲是一位卡车司机，古德温对父亲这样的人说来说去有什么用？可古德温还是继续说来说去。

“这不是想象力，爸爸。我可以做事。我有能量。”

“晚安，儿子。”古德温的母亲说道。她是一位家庭主妇。她根本没有能量。

迄今为止，古德温跟这样的父母在一起已经生活了八年。他们诚实，勤劳，常争吵，付账，去教堂。

但是他们不相信奇迹。

古德温·布朗说自己要依命上床睡觉了。他有自己的房间，在二楼，房间里有一个双层床，古德温睡在上层，下层没人睡。古德温·布朗是独生子。

他没有像精神感应、心灵致动这样可以在夜里发的功，所以他上了床，等待明天的到来。

“什么也伤害不了我。”古德温在早餐时说道。

“太好了，亲爱的。”他的母亲回答。她又给了他一些煎饼。

“这是我的主要法力。”古德温解释道。“但是我也能快速地计算数字。我能读诗，甚至用有趣的词读那些古老的东西。”

“读书好处多。”父亲告诉他。“继续读书。”

“没有什么能伤害我。”古德温重复着，嘴里挂着半块煎饼。“你们没注意到吗？我从来没有伤口或瘀伤？”

“你是个坚强的孩子。”他父亲自豪地说。

“我怎样才能说服你呢？”古德温问道。

“再吃一块煎饼吧。”他妈妈说。

古德温像其他孩子一样上学去了。他知道，在未来，很多人都有法力。他们只是还没有意识到罢了。

古德温说：“我的身体操控能力高于常人。我正在利用人类尚未开发的潜能。”

他的父母吃饭的时候也不相信。快到向他们展示一番的时候了。古德温知道这将充满戏剧性。

星期六下午，他爬进他父亲卡车的驾驶室，打开了手套箱。他拿出父亲的枪，站在厨房门口，让父母看到。他们正在中间的房间里看电视。

“你到底拿枪要干什么？”古德温的父亲从沙发上跳了起来。

“我要向你们证明我的法力。”

“古德温，那不是玩具。”他的母亲训斥道。

“你别管，苏·安。”他父亲对她说。“我会处理的。”

古德温·布朗举起枪指着自己的头。“枪里上子弹了。”他说。“我检查过了。”

“古迪，你要干什么？”他的母亲几乎尖叫起来。

“苏·安，闭嘴！”他的父亲喊道。

古德温站在厨房的桌子旁边。他父亲站在门口。

“现在，古德温，让我们谈谈。”他说。“告诉我出了什么事。”

古德温只是笑了笑。“没事，爸爸。我在展示我的一个法力，就是这样。我的最佳法力。”

“哦，上帝！”他的妈妈喊道。

“古德温，你为什么要伤害自己？”他的父亲说道。

“我不会受伤的。”古德温说道。“我会安然无恙。我顺便告诉你们：什么都不会伤害我。”

“不要犯浑。”他的父亲责备他。

“我知道你们永远不会相信我的。”古德温说。“所以我能做给你们看。”

他的胳膊举累了，于是把枪稍微放了放，随即放回了原来的位置。“古德温，你是个好孩子，”他父亲说道，“一个真正的好孩子。”

“这我知道，”古德温说道，“我只想给你们展示我的法力，这样你们就会相信我了。”

他们看起来吓坏了，古德温怀疑就算事后他们能否相信自己还不一定呢。

“这支枪不会伤害我，因为我相信自己。”古德温解释道。“在未来世界里，他们就能理解这类事情。意志力与一切事物同在，只要你认为不会，就不会有坏事发生。我就不相信坏事会发生。”

“我儿子疯了！”古德温的母亲说道。

“闭嘴，苏·安。”古德温的父亲说道。

接着，他又转而对古德温说：“我怎么才能说服你不要这样？”

“他才八岁！”古德温的母亲哭着说道。

“只要你们相信，你们就会知道我不会有事。”古德温对自己唯一的双亲说道。“到了人性相信自身的时候了，可以从你们俩开始。”

“他说话像个疯子。”古德温的母亲说道。“我的儿子鬼上身了！”

“你这么说也没有用，”古德温说道，“我马上就给你们展示我所说的。”

“儿子，不要！”他的父亲绝望地喊道。“我们会相信你的。我们从现在开始相信你，相信你有法力。你什么都不用证明。”

他们的确装出相信的样子了，古德温心想，这就是我的父母。多么愚蠢。我不会受伤的，他们怕什么？古德温·布朗把枪摁到了太阳穴上。他的父母都尖叫起来。

知道自己不会有事，古德温扣动了扳机。

Write Your Own Ending

"I do have them. Whether you believe me or not."

Goodwin Brown lived in the future. Unfortunately, his parents did not.

"With that imagination," his father said, "maybe you should go to Hollywood someday."

Goodwin's father was a truck driver. What was the use of Goodwin repeating himself to such a man? Goodwin did it anyway.

"It's not my imagination, Dad. I can do things. I have powers."

"Goodnight, son," Goodwin's mother said. She was a housewife. She hadn't any powers at all.

For eight years now, Goodwin had lived with these parents. They were honest, hard-working people who argued a lot, paid their bills, and went to church.

But they still didn't believe in miracles.

Goodwin Brown reported to bed, as ordered. He had his own room, on the second floor, with a set of bunk beds. Goodwin slept in the top bunk. No one slept in the bottom. Goodwin Brown was an only child.

He didn't have the kind of powers you could practice at night, like telepathy or psychokinesis. So he just went to bed, and waited for tomorrow.

"Nothing can hurt me," Goodwin announced at breakfast.

"That's nice, dear," his mother replied. She gave him some more pancakes.

"That's my main power," Goodwin explained. "But I can calculate numbers pretty fast, too. And I can read poetry, even that old stuff with funny words."

"Reading is good," his father told him. "Keep on reading."

"Nothing can hurt me," Goodwin repeated, with half a pancake hanging from his mouth. "Haven't you noticed that? I've never had a cut or a bruise."

"You are a tough kid," his father spoke proudly.

"How can I convince you?" Goodwin asked.

"Have another pancake," his mother said.

Goodwin went to school like any other kid. He knew that, in the future, a lot of people had powers. They just hadn't recognized them yet.

"I'm operating above the norm," Goodwin said. "I'm utilizing Mankind's untapped potential."

His parents didn't believe him at dinner, either. It was getting near time for a demonstration. Goodwin knew it would need to be a dramatic one.

On Saturday afternoon, he climbed into the cab of his father's truck and opened the glove compartment. He took out his father's gun. Standing in the kitchen doorway, he showed the gun to his parents. They were watching TV in the middle room.

"What the hell are you doing with that?" Goodwin's father leapt off the sofa.

"I'm going to prove to you my powers."

"Goodwin, that's not a toy," his mother scolded.

"Stay out of this, Sue Ann," his father said to her. "I'll handle it."

Goodwin Brown raised the gun and pointed it at his own head. "It's loaded," he said. "I checked."

"Goodie, what are you doing!" his mother almost screamed.

"Sue Ann, shut up!" his father shouted.

Goodwin stood near the kitchen table. His father stood in the doorway.

"Now, Goodwin, let's talk," he said. "Tell me what's the matter."

Goodwin just smiled. "Nothing, Dad. I'm showing you one of my powers, that's all. My best one."

"Oh, Lord Jesus Christ!" his mother shouted.

"Goodwin, why do you want to hurt yourself?" his father said.

"I won't be hurt," Goodwin said. "I'll be fine. I told you all along: nothing can hurt me."

"Don't be ridiculous," his father scolded him.

"I knew you wouldn't ever believe me," Goodwin said. "So I had to do this."

He lowered the gun for a second because his arm was getting tired. Then he put it right back. "Goodwin, you're a good boy," his father said. "A real good kid."

"I know that," Goodwin said. "I'm just showing you my power. Then you'll believe me."

The way they looked so scared, Goodwin wondered if they would believe him, even afterward.

"This gun can't hurt me because I believe in myself," Goodwin explained. "In the future they understand these things. Willpower can accomplish anything. Nothing bad happens, unless you think it's going to. I don't believe in bad things."

"My son is crazy!" Goodwin's mother said.

"Shut up, Sue Ann," Goodwin's father said.

Then, to Goodwin: "How can I talk you out of this?"

"He's only eight years old!" his mother cried.

"If you had any faith, you'd know I'd be fine," Goodwin Brown told his only parents. "It's about time that humanity started believing in itself. It may as well begin with the two of you."

"He's talking like a weirdo," Goodwin's mother said. "My

son is possessed by the devil!"

"There's no use talking anymore," Goodwin said. "I'll just show you what I mean."

"Son, don't!" his father shouted in desperation. "We'll believe you. We'll believe you from now on, about your powers. You don't have to prove anything."

They sure made a show of it, Goodwin Brown thought, these parents of mine. It was all so silly. He couldn't be hurt. What were they so afraid of? Goodwin Brown pressed the gun against his temple. Both of his parents screamed.

Knowing he'd be fine, Goodwin pulled the trigger.

朱尔斯老师的包裹

体育老师路易斯的眉头皱了起来。

校园里一团糟，到处都是铅笔和纸片，他感到奇怪：这些垃圾都是从哪里来的呢？唉，我才不愿意捡垃圾！

捡垃圾也不是他的工作。他的工作是在午饭和休息时间给孩子们传球，同时保证孩子们别一个要了另一个的命。

他叹了口气，然后开始收拾起来，他爱威塞德学校的每一个孩子，他不愿意让他们在又脏又乱的操场上玩耍。

就在他捡铅笔和纸片的时候，一辆大卡车驶进了停车场。它鸣笛两次，接着又是两次。

路易斯向大卡车跑去。“安静！”他低声说道。“孩子们在那里用功学习呢！”他边说边用手指了指学校。

一个发型蓬松、头发浓密的小个子男人从卡车上下来。“我来给一个名叫朱尔斯老师的人送包裹。”他说道。

“交给我好啦。”路易斯答道。

“你是朱尔斯老师吗？”来人问道。

“不是。”路易斯答道。

“我要把包裹给朱尔斯老师。”来人说道。

路易斯想了想，他不想让来人打扰孩子们，他知道孩子们学习的时候多么讨厌被打扰。

“我就是朱尔斯老师。”

“可你刚才不是说你不是吗？”来人问道。

“我改主意了。”路易斯答道。

来人从卡车上取了包裹，递给路易斯。“给你，朱尔斯老师。”他说道。

“嗬！”路易斯咕哝了一声，这包裹可不轻，四面都注明了“易碎品”，他还得小心谨慎，别摔了。

这个包裹太大了，路易斯都不知道自己在往哪儿走。幸好，他凭记忆记得朱尔斯老师的班在哪里，直直往前走就是。

威塞德学校是一个三十层高的高层，每层只有一个房间，朱尔斯老师的班在顶层，那也是路易斯最喜欢的班。

他推开学校的门，然后开始爬楼梯，没有电梯。

有楼梯通向地下室，但是没有人下去过，地下室有死老鼠。

箱子贴着路易斯的脸，压着路易斯的鼻子，尽管如此，他爬到第15层时，还是能闻到自助餐厅里穆什小姐做饭的香味，闻起来像是在做蘑菇。也许我可以在下楼时路过穆什小姐的房间买点儿蘑菇，他想着。他可不想错过穆什小姐的蘑菇，那可是她的拿手好菜啊。

他气鼓鼓地抱怨着，继续爬楼。他的四肢都很酸痛，可他不想歇脚，这个包裹也许很重要，他想：我要尽快给朱尔斯老师送过去。

他轻松地从第18层上了第20层，因为没有第19层。

扎夫斯小姐教的班在第19层。扎夫斯小姐不在。

最后，他挣扎地上了第30层，用头敲朱尔斯太太的门。

朱尔斯太太正在班里讲重力，这时听到了敲门声。“进来。”她大声说道。

“我开不开门。”路易斯气喘吁吁地说道。“我腾不出手。我有一个包裹要给你。”

朱尔斯老师转过身来看着全班同学。“谁愿意给路易斯开门？”她问道。

所有孩子都举起了手，学习的时候，他们很愿意被打断。

“哦，天哪，我选谁好呢？”“我要选得公平。我知道啦！我们来拼写单词比赛吧，谁拼对了谁去开门。”

路易斯又用头敲了敲门。“东西很沉。”他抱怨道。“我已经累得不行了。”

“就一秒钟。”朱尔斯老师大声回应道。“艾莉森，你拼第一个词，沉。”

艾莉森说：“H-E-A-V-Y。Heavy。”

“非常好。詹森，你拼下一个词，疲劳。”

詹森说道：“S-L-E-E-P-Y。Tired。”

路易斯感到手指汗津津，箱子就要从手上滑落了，他把箱子平衡了一下，抓紧了些。箱子的一角落入了他的臂弯，他感到手都麻了。

其实，他都没有感觉到双手已经麻木了。

“詹妮，包裹。”

詹妮说：“B-O-X。Package。”

“好极啦！”朱尔斯老师说。

路易斯感觉自己要昏过去了。

最后，约翰开了门。“拼写单词比赛我赢了，路易斯！”他说道。

“非常好，约翰。”路易斯低声说。

“你不跟我握握手吗？”约翰问道。

路易斯把箱子换到一只胳膊上，迅速握了握约翰的手，然后又一把抱住箱子，踉踉跄跄地进了教室。

“放哪儿，朱尔斯老师？”他问道。

“我不知道。”朱尔斯老师答道。“这是什么？”

“我不知道。”路易斯说。“我得先把它放下，你才能打开看是什么。”

“可是在不知道这是什么东西之前，我怎么能告诉你应该将它放哪儿？”朱尔斯老师说道。“你可能会放错地方。”

于是，路易斯抱着箱子，朱尔斯老师站在他身旁的一把椅子上扯开了箱子。路易斯的腿在颤抖。

“是一台电脑！”朱尔斯老师喊道。

学生们异口同声发出了嘘声。

“怎么回事？”路易斯问道。“我还以为电脑是万人迷呢。”

“我们不想要电脑，路易斯。”培根说道。

“搬回去吧，杰克。”特伦斯说道。

“把那个垃圾从这里带走。”莫里西亚说道。

“好啦，别这样。”朱尔斯老师说道。“电脑对我们学习是有帮助的，电脑比纸笔快多啦。”

“可是，我们学得越快，要做的就越多。”托德抱怨说。

“路易斯，你把它放在那里的台子上好啦。”朱尔斯老师说道。

路易斯把电脑放到了挨着沙里书桌的台子上，随即瘫倒在地上。

“现在，走近观察一下。”朱尔斯老师说道。

大家都围拢在电脑周围。这台电脑配备了一个全色显示器和两个磁盘驱动器。

朱尔斯老师把电脑推出了窗外。

大家都看着电脑落下去，在人行道上摔成碎片。

“看到了吗？”朱尔斯老师说道，“这就是重力。”

“哦，我现在终于明白了！”乔恍然大悟。

“谢谢你，路易斯。”朱尔斯说道。“我这一上午都在给他们讲重力，我们用铅笔和纸当例子，可是电脑下落的速度快多了。”

A Package for Mrs. Jewls

Louis, the yard teacher, frowned.

The school yard was a mess. There were pencils and pieces of paper everywhere. How would all this junk get here? He wondered. Well, I'm not going to pick it up!

It wasn't his job to pick up garbage. He was just supposed to pass out the balls during lunch and recess, and also make sure the kids didn't kill each other.

He sighed, then began cleaning it up. He loved all the children at Wayside School. He didn't want them playing on a dirty playground.

As he was picking up the pencils and pieces of paper, a large truck drove into the parking lot. It honked its horn twice, then twice more.

Louis ran to the truck. "Quiet!" he whispered. "Children are trying to learn in there!" He pointed at the school.

A short man with big, bushy hair stepped out of the truck. "I have a package for somebody named Mrs. Jewls," he said.

"I'll take it," said Louis.

"Are you Mrs. Jewls?" asked the man.

"No," said Louis.

"I have to give it to Mrs. Jewls," said the man.

Louis thought a moment. He didn't want the man disturbing the children. He knew how much they hated to be interrupted when they were working.

"I'm Mrs. Jewls," he said.

"But you just said you weren't Mrs. Jewls," said the man.

"I changed my mind," said Louis.

The man got the package out of the back of the truck and gave it to Louis. "Here you go, Mrs. Jewls," he said.

"Uhh!" Louis grunted. It was a very heavy package. The word FRAGILE was printed on every side. He had to be careful not to drop it.

The package was so big, Louis couldn't see where he was going. Fortunately, he knew the way to Mrs. Jewls's class by heart. It was straight up.

Wayside School was thirty stories high, with only one room on each story. Mrs. Jewls's class was at the very top. It was Louis's favorite class.

He pushed through the door to the school, then started up the stairs. There was no elevator.

There were stairs that led down to the basement, too, but nobody ever went down there. There were dead rats living in the basement.

The box was pressed against Louis's face, squashing his nose. Even so, when he reached the fifteenth floor, he could smell Miss Mush cooking in the cafeteria. It smelled like she was making mushrooms. Maybe on my way back I'll stop by Miss Mush's room and get some mushrooms, he thought. He didn't want to miss Miss Mush's mushrooms. They were her specialty.

He huffed and groaned and continued up the stairs. His arms and legs were very sore, but he didn't want to rest. This package might be important, he thought. I have to get it to Mrs. Jewls right away.

He stepped easily from the eighteenth story to the twentieth. There was no nineteenth story.

Miss Zarves taught the class on the nineteenth story. There was no Miss Zarves.

At last he struggled up the final step to the thirtieth story. He knocked on Mrs. Jewls's door with his head.

Mrs. Jewls was in the middle of teaching her class about gravity when she heard the knock. "Come in," she called.

"I can't open the door," Louis gasped. "My hands are full. I have a package for you."

Mrs. Jewls faced the class. "Who wants to open the door for Louis?" she asked.

All the children raised their hands. They loved to be

interrupted when they were working.

"Oh dear, how shall I choose?" asked Mrs. Jewls.

"I have to be fair about this. I know! We'll have a spelling bee. And the winner will get to open the door."

Louis knocked his head against the door again. "It's heavy," he complained. "And I'm very tired."

"Just a second," Mrs. Jewls called back. "Allison, the first word's for you. Heavy."

"H-E-A-V-Y. Heavy." said Allison.

"Very good. Jason, you're next. Tired."

"S-L-E-E-P-Y. Tired." said Jason.

Louis felt the package slipping from his sweaty fingers. He shifted his weight to get a better grip. The comers of the box dug into the sides of his arms. He felt his hands go numb.

Actually, he didn't feel them go numb.

"Jenny, package."

"B-O-X. Package." said Jenny.

"Excellent!" said Mrs. Jewls.

Louis felt like he was going to faint.

At last John opened the door. "I won the spelling bee, Louis!" he said.

"Very good, John," muttered Louis.

"Aren't you going to shake my hand?" asked John.

Louis shifted the box to one arm, quickly shook John's hand, then grabbed the box again and staggered into the room.

"Where do you want it, Mrs. Jewls?" he asked.

"I don't know," said Mrs. Jewls. "What is it?"

"I don't know," said Louis. "I'll have to put it down some place so you can open it."

"But how can I tell you where to put it until I know what it is?" asked Mrs. Jewls. "You might put it in the wrong place."

So Louis held the box as Mrs. Jewls stood on a chair next to him and tore open the top. His legs wobbled beneath him.

"It's a computer!" exclaimed Mrs. Jewls.

Everybody booed.

"What's the matter?" asked Louis. "I thought everyone loved computers."

"We don't want it, Louis," said Eric Bacon.

"Take it back, Jack," said Terrence.

"Get that piece of junk out of here," said Maurecia.

"Now, don't be that way," said Mrs. Jewls. "The computer will help us learn. It's a lot quicker than a pencil and paper."

"But the quicker we learn, the more work we have to do," complained Todd.

"You may set it over there on the counter, Louis," said Mrs. Jewls.

Louis set the computer on the counter next to Sharie's desk. Then he collapsed on the floor.

“Now watch closely,” said Mrs. Jewls.

Everyone gathered around the new computer. It had a full-color monitor and two disk drives.

Mrs. Jewls pushed it out the window.

They all watched it fall and smash against the sidewalk.

“See?” said Mrs. Jewls. “That’s gravity.”

“Oh, now I get it!” said Joe.

“Thank you, Louis,” said Mrs. Jewls. “I’ve been trying to teach them about gravity all morning. We had been using pencils and pieces of paper, but the computer was a lot quicker.”